CW01464593

# CONTENTS

# HI GUYS,

Thanks so much for joining me in my new cookbook. I am so happy to be able to share my knowledge, passion and expertise with you, as you make the steps towards leading healthier and happier lives through real food. And I will let you in on a little secret: it's super easy! My previous book, *Eat Clean*, was the beginning of a new chapter and a fantastic starting point for a series of books that are all designed to get you guys back in the kitchen, cooking with real ingredients in a way that makes your tastebuds, mind and body sing.

I truly believe that health starts in the kitchen. The moment we take that empowering step to invest love, positivity and effort into what we eat, we are taking a massive leap towards living a life that's the best version of us. When we allow ourselves to live to our full potential, things seem to get easier and life just flows. We have more energy, there is a brightness in our eyes and a fire within that enables us to start believing anything is possible. As soon as we begin to understand the profound effects food has on how we feel, look and perform, then we can make decisions that allow us to thrive as individuals and prosper in so many elements of our lives.

I've written *Healthy Made Easy* to showcase the abundance of delicious recipes you can create with minimal ingredients, time restrictions and budget constraints, without skimping on incredible flavours and optimal nutrition. But most of all, I want to show you that living a healthy lifestyle and cooking epic, healthy food is wonderfully easy! I have front-loaded this new book with tips, tricks, kitchen hacks and need-to-knows, so you're covered when it comes to getting amazing results in the kitchen in no time at all.

When it comes down to it, I believe that absolutely everybody can cook. And what's more, it can be fun, fuss free and stress free. I am by no means a trained chef and nor do I profess to be. I am simply a guy who loves to create healthy meals that everyone can enjoy. So, I want you to know that you don't have to consider yourself brilliant in the kitchen, you simply have to have a go! The moment you jump in and get your hands dirty is the moment the magic starts to happen. You will begin to experiment with new and exciting flavours and different methods of preparation, and before long you will have a whole new repertoire of recipes to nourish yourself and share with loved ones. Just imagine, if you cook two new recipes from this book per week, after a year you'll have an amazing recipe library in your head of over 140 new dishes that you can whip up on any occasion, not to mention the awesome new skills you will have developed – you will rule your kitchen! Be sure to make it fun, think positively and always believe in yourself.

One thing I often like to share with people, whether they're embarking on a new healthy way of life for the first time or they have been eating clean for yonks, is that at the end of the day you are the one in the driving seat of your own health and happiness. There's no such thing as a quick fix; there is no magic pill that will turn your life around in an instant. No-one can do this for us, and we should always do it for the right reasons. Living your best life is about small, sustainable, incremental changes each and every day that, when combined, lead to lifelong healthy habits that get easier over time. So, if you want to eat the most nutrient-dense foods available and live an amazing life, this is the cookbook for you!

I've tried to include something for everyone in this book, so make sure you get among each and every chapter. There's an array of smoothies, shots, elixirs and hot drinks to quench your thirst any time of the day. I've got your breakfasts sorted, with recipes suitable for those busy weekday mornings but also a bunch of more indulgent weekend options. I've focused lunch around things you can take to both school and the workplace, as this is often where we slip up when trying to make healthier choices. You can ditch those take-away menus on the fridge, because I've got you covered with speedy suppers that you can cook and get on the table in next to no time at all: #winning! Say goodbye to doing the dishes with my one-pan wonder recipes and cook your way through surf, turf and grown and gathered, where I've catered for carnivores and herbivores alike with multiple options from paleo to vegan and everything in between! And don't forget my sweet-treat sensations: the most nutrient-dense and delicious healthy desserts you ever have seen.

Now let's clarify some common kitchen misconceptions that I often get asked about. First of all, you don't need to stick to every single recipe as it is written. Cooking should be all about fun and flexibility, so if you're missing an ingredient simply swap it out for something similar or omit it altogether. It's okay, everything will be fine. Our creativity often reveals itself the most when we are put under pressure. I know some of my best recipes are invented when I am forced to improvise in the kitchen. Being happy to cook with scraps and leftovers is another important step in making healthy easy. A dinner made with whatever is left in the crisper or at the back of the fridge can often be the most delicious and rewarding. Especially if it prevents wastage and brings out the inner Masterchef in you. Consider it a mystery-box challenge where you have to come up with something based on what you've got on hand.

When possible, share your creations with loved ones – whether it's cooking one of my quick and easy mid-week suppers for the family or making a sweet treat to take to work to encourage healthier eating habits. I love seeing your creations, too, so be sure to take pictures of your dishes and use the hashtag #HealthyMadeEasy, so I can double tap your photos on social media!

As I touched on above, I am not a chef, so I am not going to bore you with cheffy things like hundreds of ingredients, time-wasting steps and processes, and complicated flavours you've never heard of. I am all about the combination of epic ingredients with simple flavours that speak for themselves on the plate. How many cookbooks have you purchased that have incredible-looking pictures, but you never cook anything from them? Yep, I've got a few of those, too. This is the book you can cook from every night of the week, and rest assured you will not spend hours slaving in the kitchen, nor will it cost you an arm and a leg at the checkout! Healthy food is something we all have the right to enjoy, and this book is designed to bring you restaurant-quality flavours on a budget.

I hope that every page in this book brings you immense joy – whether it's the adventure of heading to your local market to search out yummy ingredients, the kitchen shenanigans while you prepare your food or the simple satisfaction of sitting down to a mouth-watering dish that tastes as good as it looks. My final words are that I want you to promise me that you'll back yourself, give everything a go and enjoy the journey with a smile on your face. Don't forget it's not how good you are at something, it's how much fun you have doing it.

LUKE
xx

# THE KNOWLEDGE

I love this section of the book. It's a guide to how you can make your cooking as easy and enjoyable as possible, and the food you eat the tastiest and most nutritious it can be. It's also full of tips and tricks that will help you save time and money. What's not good about that?

## Keep it simple, sexy

'Cooking should be difficult and complicated', said no-one, ever! Food doesn't have to be stressful and time-consuming – this book is all about maximum health and flavour with minimum time and effort. I understand we all live very busy and stressful lives at times, but following a healthy lifestyle and preparing good food shouldn't be a difficult addition to our current workload or life's pressures. So my advice is to keep it simple, sexy. Whether it's sautéing some greens with a little chilli and garlic or just reheating last night's leftovers, simplicity is often the key to sustaining a healthy and happy lifestyle.

## Cook in bulk

This is an amazing way to save time and money, and minimise waste. Firstly, whipping up a large batch of one dish means less time spent in the kitchen with more food to show for it. Secondly, when we cook like this we tend to use up all of our ingredients and leave minimal scraps. Take a good hearty bolognese, for example; you can make a big batch of this bad boy and use up heaps of ingredients you have lying around the kitchen that might normally get ditched, such as that bendy carrot, lonely brown onion or odd garlic clove lurking at the back of the fridge. Finally, buying ingredients in bulk is often cheaper than shopping every day for small quantities, so don't be afraid to shop big knowing it will stretch over a number of days.

## Prep like a boss

I learnt this term from my mate Joe Wicks, the Body Coach. We toured together last year, and one of his catchphrases was 'prep like a boss', which basically means spending a bit of time prepping your food for the week ahead – whether that's batch-cooking some meals in advance for taking to work or having certain foods prepped and ready to go for when you're short on time. Pop these foods into plastic containers and refrigerate or freeze them, so that you have plenty of healthy options for the days ahead.

## Make it market fresh

We get our vitality from our food, which means it's important that we always have something fresh and full of nature's wonderful energy as part of each meal – even if it's just a few spinach leaves chucked in at the end! Seek out your nearest fresh-food market – the food will be fresher, often pesticide-free and maybe even organic. And by going at the end of the day, you can stock up on heaps of produce at make-you-smile low prices.

## Choose cheap cuts

Eating healthily shouldn't be expensive. One of the easiest ways to save on your weekly grocery bill is to opt for alternative choices of animal protein over the standard cuts of meat. These different cuts are usually cheaper and – being full of the good-quality animal fats we should be celebrating in our diet – are also often the most nutritious. Plus, as these cuts generally require longer cooking, they will introduce you to different techniques, such as slow cooking and pressure cooking, that not only deliver delicious results but also help reduce the actual time you have to spend in the kitchen!

### Learn to be supermarket savvy

The best bit of advice I can give if you are shopping at the supermarket is to shop towards the 'outside' of the store – which means the aisles containing fresh fruit and vegetables, cold fridges with the meats, poultry and seafood, and the sections that store nuts, seeds, herbs and spices. If what you're buying doesn't require a packet then that's great (as it means you're picking up something fresh and delicious!) but if it does, always be sure to read the labels. While the front of the tin might say 'natural coconut cream', for example, it might still contain added preservatives, thickening agents and other nasties. It may sound time-consuming, but it only takes a few seconds per item, and you'll get to know the good brands pretty quickly.

### Stock up on stocks

Stocks and broths are making a comeback baby, and rightfully so! Not only do they form the delicious, flavoursome base of so many meals and sauces, they are also incredibly healing for our gut – the collagen in stocks made from good-quality animal bones repairs the lining of our stomach and delivers an abundance of nutrients unlike anything else. Stocks can be made from virtually any animal bones, and it's always fun trying different vegetables, herbs and spices to mix up the flavour combinations.

### Ditch the dishes

One thing that can hold people back from getting in the kitchen is the clean-up that follows, and that's partly why I've created my One-Pan Wonders chapter (see pages 151–173), as there's nothing better, or cleaner, than preparing an entire meal using just one main pan or dish. It cuts down on cleaning up after yourself – which in itself saves a lot of time and water – plus it also allows all the flavours of whatever you are cooking to develop together into something truly fantastic.

### Eat everything

Minimising waste not only saves us money, it also helps us do our bit to reduce our impact on the planet, which can only be a good thing, right? It is about using what you have, celebrating leftovers and finding a way to use up every last element of your produce – from the peel, pith, stalks and stems of your fruit and veg, to the bones and trimmings of your meat. It's one reason I love using offal, as it means no part of the animal is wasted, and we are making a respectful choice when choosing to eat meat. Think of it as a challenge, and try to do the right thing for yourself and the environment from the moment you start shopping – your wallet (and the world) will thank you.

### Celebrate the seasonal

If you can't find a certain ingredient when you're shopping, it probably means it isn't in season. And guess what? That's okay! Try to be adaptable and see if you can find similar, if not better, seasonal substitutes for your recipe that are of similar nutritional value. The fewer carbon miles our food has to travel before it hits our plate, the better it tastes and the better it is for the environment. It'll also be cheaper, making it a win-win in my book!

### Leave stress at the door

Food and stress should never, ever go together – it's not a healthy combination. Whether it's the stress surrounding the preparation of a dish or perhaps the unhealthy relationship we can develop with certain types of foods, do your best to leave it at the door. Follow my kitchen hacks (see page 12) and try to remember that food is one of the most glorious, simple pleasures in life that has the power to make us feel wonderful.

# TOP 10 KITCHEN HACKS

Here is my definitive list of hacks to help make the kitchen your favourite room in the house. Follow these simple steps, and I can assure you that cooking will become an easy, seamless experience – you can thank me later when you're scoring 10 out of 10 from your housemates or pets!

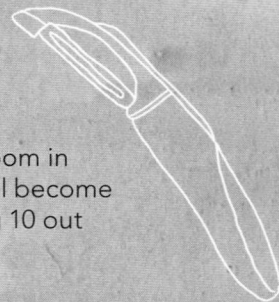

## 1. Start clean and tidy

Stepping into a clean, tidy kitchen is a key starting point for making healthy cooking easy. Cooking surrounded by mess and clutter is only going to lead to a stressed you, and then that stress ends up on the plate! So take the bills, kids' homework, pet food and batteries off the kitchen bench before you begin (and don't even get me started on those takeaway menus).

## 2. Equip yourself properly

There's nothing worse than getting halfway through a recipe and realising your vegetable peeler is completely covered in rust, or that you can't find the lid to the food processor. I know that when I hit these types of obstacles it derails my cooking, so don't let it interfere with yours. Invest in a really good set of basic appliances and utensils that you know will see you through this awesome health journey. Wash them, store them properly and look after them – you are the tradie and they are the tools you need to bring it all together. Start with good knives, quality chopping boards and a strong food processor and build from there.

## 3. Plan, sort and prioritise your shop

Organising the food shopping is one of my favourite kitchen hacks but it is often overlooked. Firstly, always plan your shop. How many times have you wandered down the supermarket aisles convinced there was one last thing you needed, only to remember it when you put the key in the front door? Hello, I hear ya! So always take a list with you. (Also, treat every recipe you follow like Santa's Christmas list, and check it twice to make sure you've got everything.) Secondly, when the complete shop does make it to the kitchen bench, sort through your ingredients! Separate them into items you can half-prep now (see point 4), and things that need to go in the fridge or pantry straight away, then sort the foods in order of use-by date. This is especially useful for common perishables like meat, celery and eggs (who needs three half-empty cartons anyway?). Now when you open the fridge and pantry doors, you will see what needs to be used up first and will remember to cook it before it needs the chuck!

## 4. Get bagging those veggies

I love using zip-lock, snap-lock and press-together-with-your-finger bags! I always portion up my broccoli and cauliflower florets, carrots and sweet potatoes for future use. Place them into single-serve packets or the desired amount needed for you and your loved ones, and pop them in the freezer. They'll never go bad and be wasted, plus when you are short on time it means half your prep is already done. You can use frozen vegetables for stocks, broths and soups and defrost them easily for stir-fries, roasts and grilling. #Winning!

## 5. Keep your freezer full

A full freezer is a happy freezer (trust me, mine tells me so all the time!) and having good food on hand at all times is one of the keys to making healthy eating easy. Whether it's chopped veggies that help make Monday's dinner a breeze, or the leftovers from when your mother-in-law didn't fancy seconds, a properly stocked freezer means you will never fall prey to those nondescript packets lurking at the back of the pantry. We all have days when we arrive home with no energy to cook, so let your freezer take the pressure off.

BROCCOLI
NOVEMBER 18

## 6. Create a vegetable stock bag

Sadly, not all vegetables are created equal and I see so many perfectly good ones wasted due to their colour, size or imperfections. Is this a reflection on society or simply a lack of thinking? A nutrient-rich vegetable stock is one of the best starting points for a healthy meal or sauce, and it's a great way to use them up. To make your own, simply take your imperfect picks, close-to-being-off veggies, trimmings and peelings and put them all together in a large zip-lock bag in the freezer. Then, when it's time to make a good, hearty vegetable stock you have your bounty all ready to go!

## 7. Create chicken, fish and beef bone bags

Bone broths and stocks help digestion and improve our absorption of other nutrients, so that when you eat your yummy fermented vegetables, for example, everything does what it is supposed to do. Whenever you roast a chook, bake a fish or have leftover cooked or uncooked beef, lamb or pork bones, be sure to pop them in some zip-lock bags, place them in the freezer and use them for making bone broths down the track. Also, ask your butcher for bones whenever you get the chance. (Just don't tell mine that the bones I ask for to give my dog, I actually use to make broth!)

## 8. Create a smoothie bag

I love a quick, healthy meal on-the-go, and that's where smoothies fit in – they're a fantastic option for when you're time-poor and can't fit a quick cook-up into your day, plus kids love them! I like making ready-to-go smoothie bags with everything you need in the one easy-to-blend pouch. Think leftover vegetables, fruits on the verge, as well as nuts and seeds. These can be kept in the freezer for ages (say goodbye to food wastage) then, when you're ready for that taste sensation, simply empty the contents into your blender, add your choice of water, coconut water or nut milk and blitz!

## 9. Clean up after yourself

Finishing up with a clean kitchen after cooking is just as important as starting with one. It'll make your home feel nicer, which in turn makes you feel nicer, plus it'll encourage you to get in there later to cook that next meal … or maybe whip up dessert! One little idea to keep in mind is that with many recipes you can clean up as you go. So, instead of creating the next Leaning Tower of Pisa in the sink, start soaking, rinsing and drying as you cook and you'll be surprised how easy it is to finish up!

## 10. Don't stop having fun!

I hope by now you see this whole 'fun' thing as a recurring message! There's a good reason keep I repeating myself when it comes to having fun in the kitchen. It's because when we enjoy doing something, we are more likely to want to do it more often. And if that means you guys spending more time in the kitchen cooking incredible healthy food, then I am a very happy man. Cooking is fun when we are present in the moment, when we are passionate about celebrating the most nutrient-dense foods available, and when we get to sit down and appreciate the joy it brings ourselves and those around us.

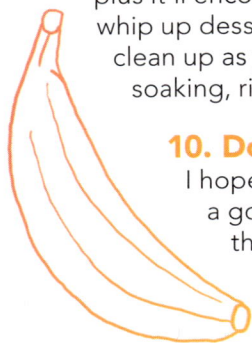

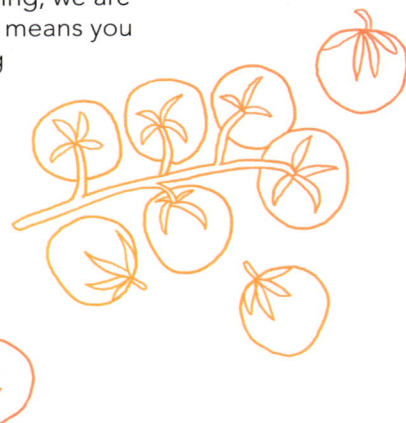

# MY 12 MUST-HAVE KITCHEN STAPLES

## Almond meal (flour)

Whether you're cooking something sweet or savoury, almond meal has you covered – it's a go-to in my house as a gluten-free flour alternative. Either source a good-quality one from the shops or make your own by blitzing raw almonds in a powerful food processor until they form a fine powder (just be sure not to take it so far it turns into nut butter!). Use almond meal in your savoury dishes to crumb, coat and batter, or try adding it to your brownies, cakes and other sweet treats like my Coconut and Blueberry Loaf (see page 64).

## Bacon

I think well-sourced, free-range, nitrate-free bacon would probably make my 'if you could only ever eat one food again' list. It's versatile, salty goodness is divine eaten on its own or added to other ingredients to help take a meal to the next level. Bacon also contains a great balance of protein and healthy fats, giving us a slow, steady release of energy. Top your salads with crispy bacon bits, add cubes of it to my Special Fried Rice (see page 152) for extra flavour or fry off rashers to make Crispy Bacon Chips (see page 192).

## Berries

I always have a packet of frozen organic berries in my freezer, and often a fresh punnet in my fridge if local and in season. Berries are a fantastic low-fructose fruit option, rich in antioxidants and bursting with flavour. Whether it's the subtle, sweet flavour of blueberries or the punch of tart raspberries, I can always find a way to get them into my day-to-day eating. Try adding berries to your morning smoothie or simply enjoy them on their own as a healthy treat when your sweet-craving alarm bells go off.

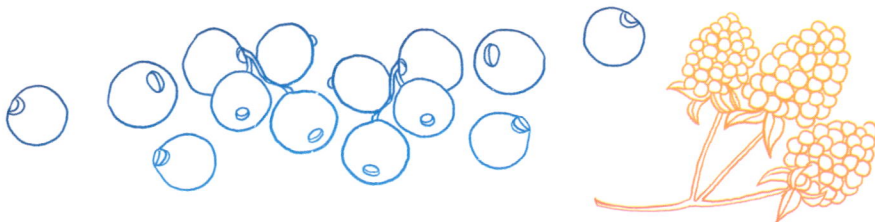

## Cacao

Cacao is basically raw chocolate before all the good stuff has been processed out. While it's packed full of antioxidants and magnesium and is highly nutritious, it's also a super-tasty and extremely versatile ingredient. It is important to note that cacao and cocoa are not the same thing. Cocoa is processed cacao with only a fraction of the nutrients retained. So, try to stick to raw cacao powder to get the most out of this ingredient's many health benefits. Add cacao powder to smoothies, combine it with warm nut milks to make delicious hot chocolate or even add a few pinches to savoury dishes like my Easy Chilli con Carne (see page 144).

## Cauliflower and broccoli

I think we could all benefit from having more vegetables in our lives, and these two are my top picks due to their many health benefits, versatility and flavour. Kept fresh or frozen, they can be the star of a meal themselves or make the perfect addition to pretty much any dish. Cauliflower and broccoli both work wonderfully in curries, stir-fries and stews, but my go-to creations involve roasting them in the oven with coconut oil and garlic until crisp, or turning them into my Breakfast Broccoli Bread or Crispy Cauli Pakoras (see pages 65 and 96).

## Cinnamon and vanilla pods

Cinnamon and fresh vanilla pods are two wonderful spices to have on hand. Cinnamon helps regulate blood-sugar levels and tricks your mind into thinking you're having something sweet, while vanilla always manages to take any homemade almond milk, breakfast smoothie or baked item to the next level. When using vanilla, it's the pod or extract that you're after – steer clear of the processed and sweetened flavouring or chemically produced essence. Cinnamon and vanilla are great added to anything sweet – think muffins, slices and drinks, such as my Hot Chilli Chocolate (see page 34).

## Coconut oil

Cold-pressed organic coconut oil is probably the most versatile ingredient in my kitchen – I use it for frying, baking, smoothies and desserts. Why do I use it so widely? Well, it's rich in medium-chain triglycerides, which are more easily absorbed into the blood than the long-chain triglycerides in other oils. This means that coconut oil is converted into energy much more easily than other oils and also helps you feel energised for longer.

## Eggs, free-range

I couldn't live without eggs! They are one of the cheapest, best-quality sources of protein available to us, containing a wide range of vitamins and minerals together with all the essential amino acids, making them a complete protein. It's best to choose organic free-range eggs – pasture-raised where possible – because happy hens produce healthy eggs. For something seriously satisfying, try my Ultimate Dinner Omelette (see page 130).

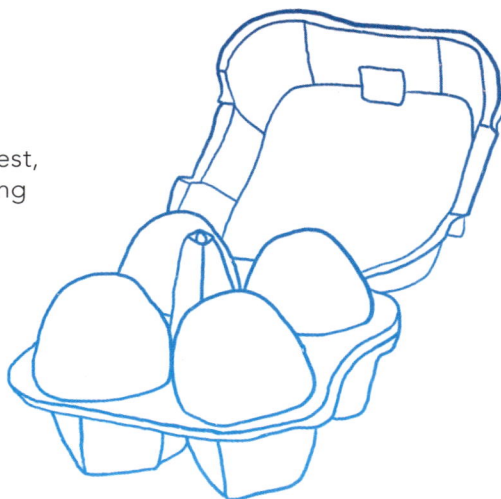

## Herbs and spices

I have always said that simple, good-quality herbs and spices can elevate a simple dish to restaurant quality – the depth of flavour and complexity they can bring to other ingredients is second-to-none. The fact that they are also rich in disease-fighting antioxidants is something of a bonus! When made into pastes, rubs and marinades, spices can help take your food on a culinary trip around the world, as my seasonings (see pages 264–265) demonstrate. Fresh herbs are great used in salads, pestos, dressings and sauces like my zesty chimichurri (see page 142), as well as scattered over dishes before serving.

## Mince, frozen

Get in the habit of always having some kind of mince in the freezer, ready for defrosting when you have one of those 'nothing left in the house' moments. It doesn't matter if you're a fan of beef, chicken or lamb, you'll thank me by stocking up on this affordable type of meat. Embrace the versatility of mince in any number of quick and easy ways – whipping it into meatballs, bangin' burgers or a beautiful bolognese. For a different way to start your day, check out my Beefed-up Shakshuka (see page 63).

## Sweet potatoes

Sweet potatoes are a wonderful source of vitamins A, B5 and B6. They are also a fantastic unprocessed, unrefined carbohydrate, making them perfect for providing that energy hit you need to start your day with, or as a post-training refuel. Have you baked or roasted a sweet potato yet? The longer you leave them in the oven, the more delicious and caramelised they become. Sweet potatoes also make awesome fritters, a great healthy 'pocket' for whatever filling you like, and can even be used in sweet recipes like my Brilliant Brownies with Blueberry Coulis (see page 240).

## Zucchini

I love zucchini as they are widely available, inexpensive and seriously versatile in the kitchen, plus they contain a surprising amount of nutritional goodness including high levels of vitamin A, vitamin C, potassium and magnesium. The most commonly found zucchini are green, but keep an eye out for the yellow ones too – they really brighten up the plate! Zucchini can be used in so many different ways: they are great incorporated into fritters, spiralised into noodles or sautéed and added to rich vegetable sauces, though it's hard to look past my Zucchini Chips with Aioli (see page 102) for a crispy, moreish snack.

# WHAT'S THE DEAL WITH ...?

I want to share some questions I am regularly asked, as I think they help to explain my approach to recipes as well as my general food philosophy. For me, it's really important to answer these questions as they help to explain the reasoning behind my choice of ingredients. They make it clear why many of my recipes are free from certain ingredients, such as dairy, grains, legumes, gluten and refined sugar, for example, while also explaining why I choose to celebrate and embrace certain foods that echo my beliefs.

It is important to note that many people may have no dietary issues with some of the below. We have a wonderful thing called bio-individuality that makes us unique in so many ways, and we need to understand that we are all different in what we can and can't consume. In the interests of the constantly changing dietary choices we are faced with – backed by our ever-evolving understanding of how food affects our bodies and minds – I have chosen to keep this book free from these common allergens and irritants. I see this as a way of helping to press the 'reset' button on our health and wellness, enabling you to move forwards into a future where you make your own decisions about what foods you enjoy and what works for you.

## What's the deal with ... grains and legumes?
Grains and legumes, including beans, all contain anti-nutrients, also referred to as enzyme inhibitors. These enzyme inhibitors make them difficult for our stomachs to digest and make it hard for us to absorb our food properly. The two most common irritants are phytic acid, which binds to minerals, preventing their full absorption, and lectins, which form part of a plant's defence system from being eaten and enter the blood unchanged. These foods are linked closely to IBS, leaky gut and autoimmune diseases. You can soak, ferment or sprout grains and legumes to reduce or remove their toxicity completely, but for the purposes of this book I have largely steered clear of using these ingredients, making it a safe place for those trying to keep these foods out of their diet and saving time on the extra preparation methods that these foods often require to make them easy to eat.

## What's the deal with ... refined sugar?
Refined sugars are highly addictive substances stripped of any of their original nutrient content, and are often referred to as 'empty calories'. I highly recommend avoiding processed and refined sugars (and all processed food options, for that matter), as they mess with your energy levels, blood-sugar regulation and appetite control. It has been proven that we lack the hormone necessary to tell the brain that we are full when eating sugar, which can lead to excessive overeating and food-addiction issues. My recipes are packed with unrefined, natural sugars that are rich in vitamins and minerals. These sugars are also always combined with a good-quality fat source, which slows the release of glucose into your blood stream, thereby helping to manage your energy, appetite and mood.

## What's the deal with ... dairy?
I'll start by saying that dairy is not as nutrient-dense as meat, fruits or vegetables (so I know what I'd rather fill my plate with). It is also highly insulinogenic – meaning it promotes the release of insulin. Also, a large number of people out there suffer from a degree of lactose intolerance, many simply not realising it but not feeling great after they consume dairy. That's why I have restricted the use of dairy in this book to high-fat, low-lactose dairy options, such as butter and ghee, for those who can tolerate it and have given alternatives for those who would rather omit dairy completely.

## What's the deal with ... gluten?

Gluten is a complex, long-chain protein that many of us struggle to digest. The inability to digest this form of protein can cause bloating and discomfort, and can interfere with the optimal digestion process and absorption of food. None of my recipes include gluten, making this book a wonderfully safe environment for anyone who may be affected. It is important to add that many gluten-free food options have many other nasty ingredients added, like artificial sweeteners, excess refined sugars and processed carbohydrates, so if you do need to be gluten free choose your food wisely or – even better – cook it for yourself!

## What's the deal with ... quinoa and buckwheat?

This is a very common question in paleo/primal circles, as neither quinoa nor buckwheat are strictly grains. They are actually both seeds but are referred to as pseudo-grains, because they can cause some similar irritations to other common grains. Both are super-high in protein, gluten free and low in toxins when prepared with care. I find these foods sit well with me nutritionally and provide me with a good source of nutrients, but, again, using them is up to you – so do what you feel works best for your body.

## What's the deal with ... vegetable and seed oils?

Vegetable and seed oils contain high levels of omega-6 fatty acids that, when over-consumed, can result in various health concerns including inflammation, which has been linked to cancer. That's why I suggest you steer clear of all vegetable and seed oils – including canola, rice bran, rapeseed, cottonseed and sunflower oil – and why in this book you will see coconut oil as the recommended cooking fat, with olive oil and avocado oil used for raw dressings and sauces. For cooking, animal fats, such as lard, tallow and duck fat and butter and ghee (for those that can tolerate them) are also great and add lots of flavour to your food.

## What's the deal with ... organic and free range?

This is a tough question because everyone is different with what they can source and afford. The first thing to do is take to the pressure off this decision, because it is an extra, unnecessary stress factor that we don't need to associate with food. If you can afford organic vegetables, and that is sustainable for your lifestyle, that's great. If, however, you are in a position where you are perhaps living week to week, purchasing any vegetables, let alone organic, can be hard enough. My advice here is to just do your best – we all have different circumstances, and it isn't anyone else's place to dictate what you should be buying. Conventional vegetables should simply be washed thoroughly. When it comes to free range, poultry and pork are non-negotiables for me, as the health of the chickens and pigs, as well as the nutrients passed on, can vary greatly depending on whether they are intensively farmed or not. I also always try to buy grass-fed or grass-finished beef where possible and choose sustainable line-caught fish to be kind to our oceans, or stick to the small oily fish – like sardines and mackerel – that we have in abundance.

# WHAT DOES A HEALTHY-MADE-EASY PLATE LOOK LIKE?

**My top 5 fuss-free secrets to make healthy eating easy**

**Keep it simple:** less really is more when it comes to ingredients.

**Keep it real:** choose real, nutrient-dense whole foods for optimum health and flavour.

**Keep on going:** never give up and stay strong – it will get easier as you establish a routine!

**Keep it fun:** you will wake up each day wanting to eat healthy food if it's fun.

**Keep the love:** love yourself, love your food and love how it makes you feel.

**WATER**
*for hydration*

**BROTH**
*for immune system support*

# FERMENTED FOODS
### for gut health

SAUERKRAUT

## ABOVE GROUND VEGETABLES

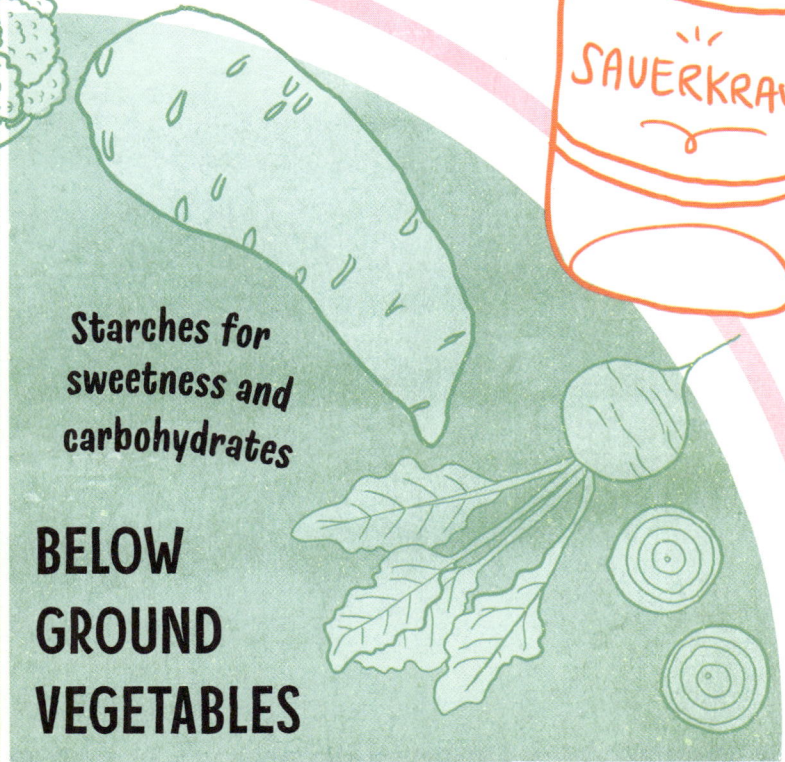

Packed with phytonutrients, colour and vibrance

## BELOW GROUND VEGETABLES

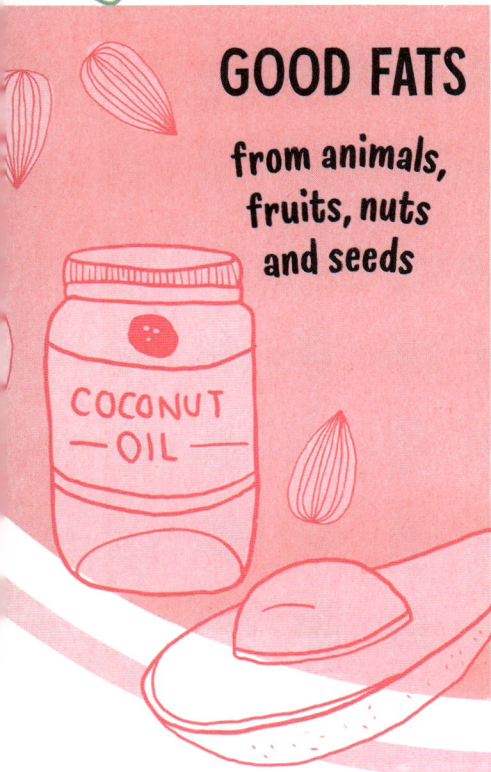

Starches for sweetness and carbohydrates

## GOOD FATS

from animals, fruits, nuts and seeds

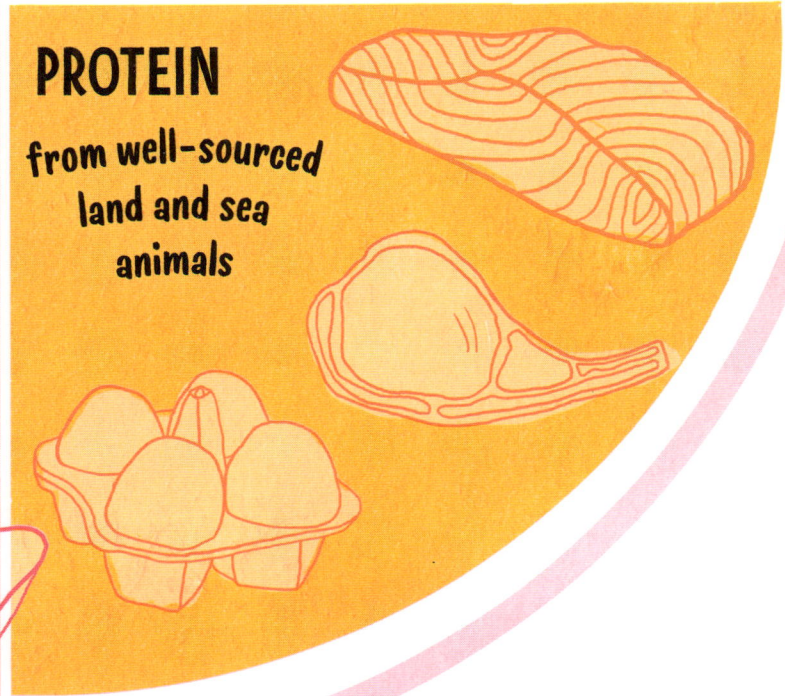

COCONUT OIL

## PROTEIN

from well-sourced land and sea animals

# DRINKS

Looking to start your day with zest, flavour and an overall cleansing sensation? Look no further than this easy-to-make morning citrus cleanser, which packs all the punch of a cold-pressed juice without wasting all the fantastic fibre usually discarded when juicing. This is a perfect drink for those looking to detox and cleanse their system all at the same time. It's the healthiest slushie you'll ever taste!

SERVES 1

# MORNING CITRUS CLEANSER

½ orange, peeled
½ lemon, peeled
½ lime, peeled
½ Lebanese cucumber
1 garlic clove
2 cm piece of ginger, peeled
4 ice cubes
filtered water, if necessary

Place all the ingredients in a food processor or high-speed blender and whiz everything together until smooth (if it's a bit thick for your liking, loosen it up with a little filtered water). Pour into a glass and serve straight away.

## TIPS

This cleanser is best enjoyed fresh before any of the ingredients oxidise. To take advantage of its incredible anti-inflammatory properties, try adding a 2 cm piece of fresh turmeric – it'll add a lovely flavour boost, too!

This morning kickstarter celebrates three of my all-time favourite ingredients: cacao, chilli and coffee. It's great to get you firing on all cylinders in the morning or as a pre-workout drink before you hit a training session! Alternatively, try pouring this over some dairy-free healthy ice cream for an amazing affogato!

SERVES 1

# CACAO, CHILLI, COFFEE KICKER

3 tablespoons fresh espresso coffee
2 teaspoons cacao powder
¼ teaspoon chilli powder
½ teaspoon coconut sugar or maple syrup, plus extra if necessary
2 teaspoons coconut oil, melted
4 ice cubes

Place all the ingredients in a food processor or high-speed blender and blitz briefly to combine. Taste, and add a little extra coconut sugar or maple syrup if you like, then blitz again until smooth. Pour into a glass and drink up.

## HEALTH BOOST

Cacao and coffee are both packed full of powerful antioxidants, while chilli powder helps boost your metabolism. The coconut oil in this kickstarter slows the release of the caffeine into your bloodstream, keeping you buzzing for longer.

When it comes to digestion, our stomach acid needs to be balanced correctly for us to be able to break down our food properly. Too little and we can wake up not feeling hungry, but too much and we can suffer from reflux and heartburn. This tonic is designed to stimulate your body's natural production of stomach acid and activate all the necessary functions in your gut for the day's meals ahead.

SERVES 1

# APPLE CIDER DIGESTION TONIC

1 teaspoon apple cider
    vinegar
2 cm piece of ginger,
    peeled
pinch of cayenne pepper
¼ teaspoon dried oregano
¼ teaspoon dried rosemary
pinch of salt
100 ml coconut water
cucumber slice, to serve

Combine all the ingredients in a food processor or high-speed blender until smooth. Pour into a glass and drink straight away – downing it in one go as a quick shot and chasing it with a generous slice of cucumber.

Packing the serious inflammation-fighting punch of turmeric, this little wellness tonic will be sure to heal and invigorate you if you're feeling run down or have a nasty cold. The lemon provides lots of energy, while the kick you get from the cayenne will help clear any congestion you might be experiencing.

SERVES 1

# TURMERIC AND CAYENNE COCKTAIL

2½ tablespoons coconut
    water, plus extra if
    necessary
1 lemon, peeled
2 cm piece of ginger,
    peeled
1 teaspoon ground turmeric
1 teaspoon coconut oil,
    melted
small pinch of cayenne
    powder (more if you like
    it hot)
pinch of salt
pinch of freshly ground
    black pepper

Place all the ingredients in a food processor or high-speed blender and whiz everything together until smooth (if it's a bit thick for your liking, or you prefer a longer drink, just loosen it up with some more coconut water). Pour into a glass and drink straight away.

Cacao, chilli, coffee kicker, page 24

Turmeric and cayenne cocktail, page 25

Apple cider digestion tonic, page 25

Morning citrus cleanser, page 24

Forgot to eat enough greens this week? Well, here's one way of getting your daily requirement in one go that can be enjoyed at breakfast, lunch, dinner, or maybe even for dessert! By whipping it up in a blender or food processor, this thick smoothie contains even more goodness than a regular green juice, where a lot of the good stuff is left behind in the pulp that gets discarded.

SERVES 1

# GREEN CRUSH

½ avocado
1 banana, frozen if possible
1 Lebanese cucumber, roughly chopped
1 handful of baby spinach leaves
1 celery stalk, chopped
1 handful of flat-leaf parsley leaves
1 handful of kale or silverbeet, stalks removed
200 ml Vanilla Almond Milk (see page 252)
200 ml coconut water, plus extra if necessary
pinch of salt
4 ice cubes

Place all the ingredients in a food processor or high-speed blender and whiz everything together until really well combined. Pour into a glass and enjoy!

## TIP

This smoothie is designed to be chewed and savoured as much as it is to be drunk straight up, but if you'd rather have it a bit thinner, simply loosen it up with some more coconut water when blending. Also, if you're getting your coconut water from a young coconut, feel free to throw some of the flesh in there, too!

I think it is really important to celebrate real food as part of a serious training regime, because so many store-bought gym-related supplements are full of nasty ingredients we don't need. So, go on, give this all-natural shake a try – it'll become your new post-workout go-to before you know it!

SERVES 1

# NATURALLY ARNOLD POST-WORKOUT SHAKE

300 ml coconut water
2 eggs
1 banana, frozen if possible
1 tablespoon peanut butter (any other nut butter is fine if you're paleo)
2 teaspoons chia seeds
1 vanilla pod, split and seeds scraped
4 ice cubes

Place all the ingredients in a food processor or high-speed blender and whiz together until really well combined. Pour into a glass and drink straight away.

## TIP

Good-quality free-range eggs, stored correctly, are safe to consume raw with a very low risk of any contamination. However, if they're not your thing, simply swap them out for 2 heaped scoops of your favourite protein powder or 2 heaped tablespoons of almond meal instead.

Time spent in the kitchen is the BEST HAPPINESS therapy.

You know those mornings when you have to run out the door with no time for breakfast? We all have them, and it's for these days that I have created this breakfast-on-the-go smoothie.

SERVES 1

# BREAKFAST-ON-THE-GO

250 ml (1 cup) Vanilla Almond Milk or Homemade Coconut Milk (see pages 252–253)
1 banana, frozen if possible
100 g blueberries, frozen if possible
1 egg
1 tablespoon almond butter
2 teaspoons honey
1 vanilla pod, split and seeds scraped
pinch of ground cinnamon
pinch of maca powder (optional)
4 ice cubes

Blitz all the ingredients in a food processor or high-speed blender until smooth. Pour into a glass and drink up!

## HEALTH BOOST

Also known as Peruvian ginseng, maca powder is a nutrient-dense whole food available in health-food stores that can help rebalance our hormones, increasing our energy levels, sex drive and focus. It's pretty powerful stuff – but this smoothie is still great without it.

## TIP

I love using frozen bananas and berries because they make smoothies nice and thick. Don't forget to peel your bananas before freezing them, as the peel is very hard to remove afterwards.

Here's the chocolate bar we all know and love, but this time made with nutrient-dense ingredients and in the form of a smoothie!

SERVES 1

# CHOC 'CHERRY RIPE' SMOOTHIE

250 ml (1 cup) Vanilla Almond Milk or Homemade Coconut Milk (see pages 252–253)
100 g frozen pitted cherries
1 tablespoon macadamia butter
1 tablespoon shredded coconut
1 tablespoon cacao powder
1 tablespoon maple syrup
1 vanilla pod, split and seeds scraped
4 ice cubes
cacao nibs, to serve

Place everything except the cacao nib in a food processor or high-speed blender and whiz together until smooth. Pour into a glass, sprinkle with a few cacao nibs and enjoy!

Breakfast-on-the-go

Choc 'cherry ripe' smoothie

# FOOD FOR FUEL

While it might sound a bit dry, understanding how food is used by the body as fuel is a really exciting and enjoyable process. It enables you to experience food on more than just a sensory level, unlocking the knowledge of how you can use it to function at your best in your everyday life. And it's understanding this link between what you eat and how you move that can make a huge impact on improving your personal health. For example, I don't believe in cutting out carbohydrates completely, as I see a very valuable place for them in our diet – instead it is about choosing the right sources at the right times. Consuming a sweet potato before bed might not be the best idea, but I would recommend having one upon waking or before exercise, so that all the wonderful, healthy energy it's packed with gets utilised by the body. Likewise, protein is a wonderful nutrient that can help build and repair our bodies, but like anything, over-consumption can lead to us storing the excess as fat, so it is about being mindful of how much we eat. Learning how particular food groups help us perform at our best helps stop us demonising them unnecessarily, and steers us towards avoiding over-consumption or undernourishment, which can make all the difference to our overall health and wellbeing.

I am a massive fan of the famous Mexican combination of chilli and chocolate. Here, the richness of cacao combines with the kick of the chilli to make an amazing base for this warming drink … just be sure to choose the heat of your chilli powder wisely!

SERVES 1

# HOT CHILLI CHOCOLATE

250 ml (1 cup) canned coconut milk
3 tablespoons filtered water
1 tablespoon cacao powder, plus extra to serve
1 teaspoon maple syrup, plus extra if necessary
½ teaspoon ground cinnamon
½ vanilla pod, split and seeds scraped
1 teaspoon chilli powder
dollop of Whipped Vanilla Coconut Cream (see page 211), to serve (optional)

Heat a small saucepan over medium heat. Add the coconut milk, filtered water, cacao powder, maple syrup, ground cinnamon, vanilla seeds and chilli powder and whisk gently, until everything is well combined and the mixture is nice and hot. Taste and whisk in a little extra maple syrup if you like things a bit sweeter. Pour into a mug, sprinkle over a little extra cacao and serve with a dollop of whipped vanilla coconut cream, if you like.

I first fell for all things 'red velvet' at the Magnolia Bakery in New York, made famous by *Sex and the City*, and the winning combo of chocolate and beetroot has been a favourite of mine ever since! This warming drink is so cosy and comforting – it's perfect for when you need to sit down and take a moment for yourself.

SERVES 1

# RED VELVET DELIGHT

300 ml Vanilla Almond Milk (see page 252)
2 tablespoons fresh beetroot juice
1 tablespoon cacao powder
1 teaspoon maple syrup, plus extra if necessary
pinch of ground cinnamon
½ vanilla pod, split and seeds scraped

Place all the ingredients in a saucepan over medium heat and whisk gently to combine. Continue to whisk until everything is nice and hot, tasting and adding a little extra maple syrup if you like things a bit sweeter. Pour into a mug and enjoy.

## TIP

You can use store-bought unsweetened beetroot juice for this, otherwise, it is simple to make beetroot juice at home by putting one through a juicer. You'll need about ½ beetroot for the 2 tablespoons required for this recipe.

This delicious caffeine-free drink combines the warming flavours of chai tea with the sweetness of honey and healing properties of turmeric, all finished off with a little sprinkle of awesome goodness in the shape of bee pollen. So, so good, you only need to try it once to fall in love with it.

SERVES 1

# GOLDEN CHAI

300 ml (1¼ cups) Vanilla Almond Milk (see page 252)
1 teaspoon honey
½ vanilla pod, split and seeds scraped
pinch of ground cinnamon
½ teaspoon ground turmeric
pinch of ground ginger
pinch of ground cloves
pinch of ground cardamom
1 teaspoon bee pollen, to serve

Heat a small saucepan over medium heat. Add the almond milk and, as it begins to warm, whisk in the remaining ingredients, except the bee pollen, until well combined. Continue to heat, whisking gently, until nice and hot, then pour into a cup or glass and sprinkle over the bee pollen to serve.

## HEALTH BOOST

The food of young honeybees, bee pollen is considered one of nature's most complete nourishing foods, as it contains nearly all the nutrients required by humans. Bee pollen is rich in proteins, amino acids, vitamins – including the full range of B vitamins – and folic acid. You can find it in most health-food stores.

Red velvet delight, page 34

Golden chai, page 35

Hot chilli chocolate, page 34

It's time we gave your morning cuppa a clean-living makeover, so here we go, welcome to your new cup of… brothee! Broths are excellent for promoting good gut health as well as being a great way of utilising leftovers. Your cup of brothee can be whatever 'flavour' you like, but if you are new to this, I recommend starting with chicken as it's just like a warming cup of chicken soup. Try swapping one of your daily coffees for a brothee and see your energy, mood and health improve. Each batch of brothee will naturally always taste slightly different, and it is the spices you add to it that will elevate it to the next level, flavour-wise. The ones I've listed below are my favourite combinations but do try and experiment with your own mixes.

MAKES 2–3 LITRES

# BRILLIANT BROTHEE

1 tablespoon apple cider vinegar
1 onion, roughly chopped
4 celery stalks, roughly chopped
2 garlic cloves, roughly chopped
about 400 g vegetables from your vegetable stock bag in the freezer (see page 12)
2 bay leaves or thyme sprigs
1 teaspoon black peppercorns

### Chicken stock base
500 g cooked or uncooked chicken carcasses (plus any extra bits you can find like the feet, necks and wings)

### Beef stock base
1–2 kg beef bones (including ribs, marrow, knuckle and neck bones, if possible)

### Fish stock base
1 kg white-fleshed fish carcasses (including heads, tailbones and offcuts)

### Flavourings (per person)
pinch of ground turmeric
pinch of ground cumin
pinch of ground coriander
a squeeze of lemon juice
pinch of salt

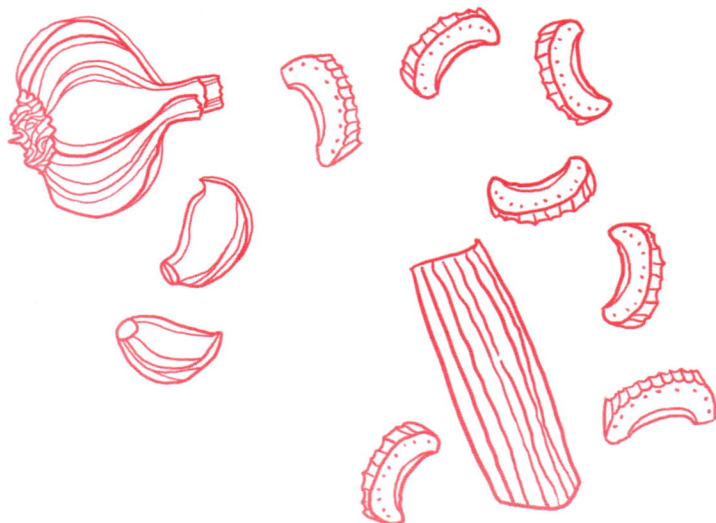

Place all the ingredients except the flavourings with your choice of stock base in a large stockpot and cover with 4 litres of water. Bring to the boil for 2 minutes and then reduce to a simmer. For chicken broth, leave to cook for at least 4 hours and up to 24 hours. For beef broth, leave to cook for at least 12 hours and up to 36 hours. For fish broth, leave to cook for at least 3 hours and up to 6 hours. The longer you cook the broth, the more minerals and nutrients you will extract from the ingredients and bones – and the darker and more richly flavoured your broth will be. Alternatively, cook your brothee in a large slow cooker on low for at least 10 hours.

Allow the brothee to cool a little, then remove the bones, strain, and transfer the liquid to suitable containers. The stock will keep for 7 days in the fridge or up to 6 months in the freezer.

When ready to use, measure out about 250 ml (1 cup) of stock per person, and ladle it into a small saucepan over medium heat. As it warms, whisk in the flavourings until well combined and continue to heat, whisking gently, until your desired temperature is reached. Pour into a cup and enjoy your delicious brothee!

## TIP

When the broth cools in the fridge the fat will congeal on the top – you can scrape this off and use it for frying in other recipes, if you like. For a simple veg stock, just simmer up all the veg ingredients without adding a meat- or fish-stock base.

## HEALTH BOOST

When heated over a long time the minerals from bones leach into the liquid they are cooked in, making them easier for us to absorb. One of the key nutrients we derive from stock is gelatine, which supports the healing of the gut lining and improves digestion by helping us better absorb the nutrients in our food.

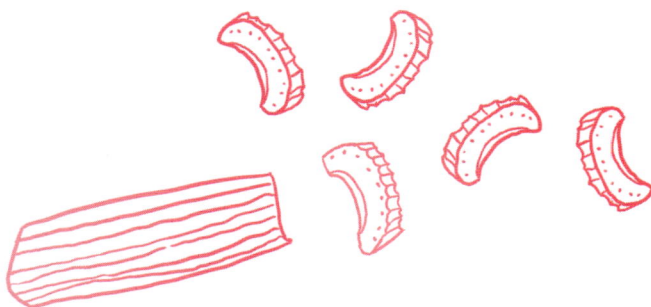

CACAO
POWDER

# BREAKFAST

This is my version of overnight oats but taken to the next level with the addition of salted caramel, which is achieved by including dates and a little salt. Who knew breakfast could be this good?

SERVES 4

# SALTED CARAMEL QUINOA BIRCHER

200 g (1 cup) quinoa, rinsed
sea salt
30 g (½ cup) shredded
   coconut
65 g almond butter
4 medjool dates, pitted
   and finely chopped
4 tablespoons chia seeds
500 ml (2 cups) Vanilla
   Almond Milk (see
   page 252)
toasted hazelnuts, roughly
   chopped, to serve
mixed berries, to serve

Bring 375 ml (1½ cups) of water to the boil in a medium–large saucepan with a lid. Add the quinoa and a generous pinch of salt. Return to the boil then immediately put the lid on, reduce the heat to the lowest setting possible and simmer gently for 15 minutes. Do not stir or move the quinoa in any way during this time. Remove the pan from the heat and let stand, still with the lid on, for up to 5 minutes. Remove the lid, gently fluff up the grains with a fork and set aside to cool.

Place 2 cups of the cooled quinoa in a large bowl (save the leftovers for a salad) along with the coconut, almond butter, dates, chia seeds, milk and another pinch of salt and mix together well, then transfer to an airtight container. Store in the fridge for up to 5 days to enjoy at your leisure throughout the week, serving each portion topped with some hazelnuts and mixed berries.

## TIP

If you love oats, this recipe is perfect for you. Simply swap out the cooked quinoa for oats and increase the almond milk slightly to make it a bit runnier and you're good to go!

Make a BIG batch to last a few days.

I love to enjoy this ultimate cafe-style breakfast in the comfort of my own home. It looks the goods and is packed full of incredible nutrient value, with the macadamia nuts in particular providing a lovely dose of the omega-3 fatty acids we need for a healthy diet. You can make all the elements in advance and store them separately, then whip up the parfaits when you're ready. Easy as!

SERVES 2

# MACADAMIA AND VANILLA GRANOLA WITH CREAMY COCONUT AND KIWI

1 quantity (1 cup) Whipped Vanilla Coconut Cream (see page 211)

2 kiwifruit (or whatever fruit is in season), peeled and diced

### Macadamia and vanilla granola

3 tablespoons coconut oil, melted

3 tablespoons maple syrup

100 g (1 cup) pecans or walnuts, crushed

100 g (⅔ cup) macadamia nuts, roughly chopped

2 tablespoons shredded coconut

125 g (1 cup) pumpkin seeds

60 g (½ cup) sunflower seeds

1 vanilla pod, split and seeds scraped

1 teaspoon ground cinnamon

Get started by preheating the oven to 200°C and lining a large baking tray with baking paper.

To make the granola, in a large bowl, combine the coconut oil and maple syrup, then add the pecans or walnuts, macadamias, shredded coconut, pumpkin seeds, sunflower seeds and vanilla seeds. Mix everything together until all the dry ingredients are well coated in the syrup mixture.

Spread the granola evenly over the baking paper and bake for 20 minutes, or until everything turns golden brown.

Remove the tray from the oven and leave to cool, then add the cinnamon and mix well.

When ready to serve, cover the base of two tall glass tumblers with a layer of the macadamia and vanilla granola, dollop over a layer of whipped coconut cream, then top with a layer of diced kiwifruit. Repeat the layers until you make it to the top of the glasses. Now dig in!

## TIP

Transfer the leftover granola (about 10 servings) to an airtight container and store for up to 2 weeks.

## HEALTH BOOST

Underneath that furry skin, kiwifruit are little nutritional powerhouses. They deliver a whole heap of antioxidants, are high in mood-boosting serotonin and each fruit contains almost twice the vitamin C of an orange.

What could be better on a weekend than indulging in a stack of delicious pancakes? This particular dish happens to be free from gluten and refined sugar but tastes so delicious the whole family will fall in love with it. I've topped these with a simple lemon–maple butter, but you can always finish them off with whatever you have in the fridge.

SERVES 2

# BANANA AND BLUEBERRY PANCAKE STACK WITH LEMON–MAPLE BUTTER

1 large banana
2 eggs
55 g (½ cup) hazelnut or almond meal
55 ml (¼ cup) coconut oil or 55 g butter, softened
30 g (⅓ cup) desiccated coconut
½ teaspoon baking powder
1 vanilla pod, split and seeds scraped
80 g (½ cup) blueberries, fresh or frozen and thawed, plus extra to serve

**Lemon–maple butter**
60 g butter, softened at room temperature
zest and juice of 1 lemon
1 tablespoon maple syrup

To make the lemon–maple butter, place all of the ingredients in a bowl, reserving a little of the lemon zest for garnish, and mix together until well combined. Transfer to the fridge to chill and firm up.

Combine the banana, eggs, hazelnut or almond meal, half of the coconut oil or butter, desiccated coconut, baking powder and vanilla seeds in a food processor and blitz to form a light, fluffy, lump-free batter. Alternatively, whisk the ingredients in a bowl by hand (just be sure to mash the banana up before you start!).

Stir in the blueberries.

Melt 1–2 tablespoons of the remaining coconut oil or butter in a frying pan over medium–low heat. Spoon 2 tablespoons of the pancake batter into the pan and spread it out a little (I like them thick so I don't spread it too much). Cook the pancake for 1–2 minutes on each side, using a spatula to carefully flip it over – when it starts to bubble on top you know it's time to give it a gentle flip. Remove from the pan and keep warm, then repeat with the remaining batter, greasing the pan lightly with more coconut oil or butter to make sure the pancakes don't stick.

To serve, pile the pancakes up as a tall stack, adding a dollop of the lemon–maple butter and a few blueberries between layers. Top with the remaining lemon–maple butter and scatter over the reserved lemon zest.

CAFE-WORTHY breakfasts at home don't get much better than these PANCAKES!

This lovely raw breakfast bowl requires no blending or cooking at all, just a simple combination of nuts, seeds, fruit and coconut oil to deliver a super-clean brekkie that will keep you full all morning.

SERVES 2

# RAW PRIMAL BOWL

1 banana
2 tablespoons tahini
2 tablespoons hemp seeds
2 tablespoons pumpkin seeds
1 tablespoon chia seeds
2 tablespoons shredded coconut
45 g (⅓ cup) finely chopped macadamia nuts
2 tablespoons coconut oil, melted
1 handful of mixed fresh berries, to serve

Place the banana and tahini in a bowl and mash together with a fork. Once really well combined, add the seeds, shredded coconut, macadamias and coconut oil and mix together well. Divide between two serving bowls, top with mixed berries and enjoy.

## HEALTH BOOST

Hemp seeds are an incredible source of healthy fats, containing a whopping 30 per cent of the good stuff! They can be found at most good health-food stores.

Packed with an epic combination of carbohydrates, good fats and protein, this one's for all the fitness junkies out there. Enjoy!

SERVES 2

# WORLD-BEATING WORKOUT BOWL

3 bananas, frozen if possible
250 ml (1 cup) Vanilla Almond Milk (see page 252)
2 tablespoons nut butter
2 tablespoons protein powder of your choice
½ avocado
1 tablespoon maple syrup
1 vanilla pod, split and seeds scraped
2–3 ice cubes

**To serve**
1 banana, finely sliced
1 tablespoon chia seeds
2 tablespoons roughly chopped macadamia nuts

Place the banana, almond milk, nut butter, protein powder, avocado, maple syrup, vanilla seeds and ice in a food processor or high-speed blender and blitz until smooth and creamy.

Divide the mixture evenly between two serving bowls and top with the sliced banana, chia seeds and macadamias. Serve straight away.

## HEALTH BOOST

If you love to supplement your daily nutrition with protein powders, then be sure you're making a smart choice with the type you pick. If you consume dairy then you can opt for a whey-based protein powder, otherwise keep an eye out for fermented brown rice or pea options. Also, be sure to read the labels carefully to make sure that the one you go for isn't full of any hidden nasties!

Rich in antioxidants and packed full of magnesium, this smoothie bowl is the perfect start to the day for all you chocolate lovers out there.

SERVES 2

# CHOCOLATE DREAM SMOOTHIE BOWL

2 bananas, frozen if possible
500 ml (2 cups) Vanilla Almond Milk (see page 252)
2 tablespoons nut butter
2 tablespoons cacao powder
1 teaspoon maple syrup
1 vanilla pod, split and seeds scraped

**To serve**
2 tablespoons shredded coconut
2 tablespoons Crunchy Cacao and Coconut Clusters (see page 56)
1 tablespoon cacao nibs
60 g fresh raspberries

Place the bananas, almond milk, nut butter, cacao powder, maple syrup and vanilla seeds in a food processor or high-speed blender and blitz until smooth and creamy.

Pour the mixture evenly into two serving bowls and top with the shredded coconut, cacao and coconut clusters, cacao nibs and raspberries. Serve straight away.

## TIP

If you're planning on enjoying this – or any of the other smoothie bowls here – solo, simply make the recipe as instructed and freeze the excess. Then, when you're ready to enjoy it later down the track, just defrost and blend briefly again, add the toppings and you're good to go.

This vibrant smoothie bowl has Hawaii written all over it! I enjoyed many bowls like this when I was over there and I wanted to share the epic summer flavours.

SERVES 2

# WAIKIKI WAKE-UP BOWL

155 g frozen blueberries
125 g frozen raspberries
1 banana, frozen if possible
2 tablespoons nut butter
250 ml (1 cup) Homemade Coconut Milk (see page 253)
1 tablespoon maple syrup
2–3 ice cubes

**To serve**
1 handful of blueberries
1 tablespoon pumpkin seeds
1 tablespoon roughly chopped brazil nuts

Place the berries, banana, nut butter, coconut milk, maple syrup and ice in a food processor or high-speed blender and blitz until smooth and creamy.

Divide the mixture evenly between two bowls and serve with the blueberries, pumpkin seeds and chopped brazil nuts.

## HEALTH BOOST

In Hawaii, smoothie bowls are often made with frozen açai berries – tiny dark berries that pack a real antioxidant punch. If you can get your hands on some (they can be found in good health-food stores), try using them to top these bowls in place of the blueberries.

Raw primal bowl, page 52

Waikiki wake-up bowl, page 53

Chocolate dream smoothie bowl, page 53

World-beating workout bowl, page 52

Who said you can't indulge in chocolate for breakfast? Certainly not me. I love this healthy, antioxidant-rich start to the day and often make up a big batch at the beginning of the week. And, not only does it make a great breakfast option, it's also great as a trail mix for school lunches or when you're on the go.

MAKES 12 SERVINGS

# CRUNCHY CACAO AND COCONUT CLUSTERS

3 tablespoons coconut oil, melted

3 tablespoons maple syrup

200 g (2 cups) walnuts or pecans, crushed

3 tablespoons shredded coconut

60 g (½ cup) cacao powder

60 g (½ cup) pumpkin seeds

60 g (½ cup) sunflower seeds

2 tablespoons cacao nibs

**To serve**

Whipped Vanilla Coconut Cream (see page 211)

fresh berries

Get started by preheating the oven to 200°C. Line a large baking tray with baking paper.

In a large bowl, combine the coconut oil and maple syrup, then add the walnuts or pecans, shredded coconut, cacao powder and the seeds. Mix everything together until all the dry ingredients are well coated in the syrup mixture.

Spread the mixture evenly over the prepared tray and bake for 20 minutes, or until everything turns golden brown.

Remove the tray from the oven, stir through the cacao nibs and leave to cool. Transfer to an airtight container and store for up to 2 weeks. To serve, top with whipped vanilla coconut cream and fresh berries.

## HEALTH BOOST

Packed with high levels of antioxidants and magnesium, cacao nibs are pieces of cacao bean that have been roasted and hulled. They taste bitter like coffee beans and have a lovely, crunchy texture, making them perfect for sprinkling over desserts and smoothie bowls.

One of the things people miss most when they cut gluten and grains from their diets is bread – without it they often don't know what to start their day with! If this sounds like you, then this recipe has your name written all over it, especially if you find yourself too short of time to make up one of my breakfast loaves (see pages 64–65). Go on, give it a go. It's quick to make and tastes fantastic.

SERVES 2

# QUICK CAULIFLOWER TOAST WITH GUAC AND EGGS

3 eggs
½ head of cauliflower, grated
sea salt and freshly ground black pepper
2 tablespoons coconut oil
80 g (⅓ cup) Gorgeous Guacamole (see page 258)
½ teaspoon chilli flakes, or to taste

Place two of the eggs in a small saucepan and cover with cold water. Cover with a lid and bring to the boil, then reduce the heat to medium and simmer gently for 3 minutes. Remove the eggs from the pan with a slotted spoon and leave to cool, then peel and set aside.

Combine the remaining egg and grated cauliflower in a large bowl. Season with salt and pepper and mix well.

Heat the coconut oil in a large frying pan over medium heat, add half of the cauliflower mixture and shape into a round patty using a spoon or spatula. Repeat to make a second patty, then fry for 4–5 minutes or until the underside of each patty is golden brown. Carefully flip the patties over and cook for a further 2–3 minutes, then remove from the pan and divide between two plates.

To serve, top each patty with the guacamole. Halve the soft-boiled eggs lengthways and place them on top, yolk-side up. Sprinkle over the chilli flakes and enjoy straight away.

# HAPPINESS

We are all striving for happiness – I'm sure I'm not alone in believing that it is what is most important in this life. Healthy food is one of the major sources of my daily happiness. I know it fuels, heals and nourishes me but, even more importantly, with its diversity of delicious options it brings me immense joy – whether that's through enjoying flavours I know and love that make me feel all warm and fuzzy inside, or as a result of expressing my intuitive creativity when cooking something for the first time. I encourage you to let food bring you similar joy – let it brighten up your day as much as it nourishes you. And if you find that poor food choices are resulting in poor mood or low energy levels, perhaps look at what small changes you can make to allow the foods you eat to become part of your happiness. Part of our journey towards happiness is removing the connection between food and unrealistic expectations. The seeking of perfection, like the quest for that bikini body or those ripped abs, can take the fun away from what we eat. Try to retain your joy for food, because when we're happy and healthy the other stuff around us just seems to fall into place. So love yourself for who you are, allow yourself to be in the right headspace for positive change, and let food play its truly magical part in that process.

Mexican flavours to start your day? Yes, please! I love this awesome recipe – it's perfect for weekend breakfasts when you have that little extra time to prepare the tortillas.

SERVES 4

# SPICY BREAKFAST BURRITOS

1 tablespoon coconut oil
250 g beef mince
1 teaspoon ground cumin
1 teaspoon ground coriander
1 teaspoon chilli flakes
2 garlic cloves, finely chopped
½ onion, finely chopped
½ red capsicum, finely diced
1 tomato, diced

### Coconut flour tortillas

3 tablespoons coconut flour
2 tablespoons arrowroot or tapioca flour
8 egg whites
zest and juice of 1 lime
generous pinch of sea salt
125 ml (½ cup) filtered water
1–2 tablespoons coconut oil

### To serve

170 g (1 cup) Gorgeous Guacamole (see page 258)
Lemon and Smoked Paprika Aioli (see page 258)
2 handfuls of baby rocket leaves
4 soft-boiled eggs, peeled and halved

Melt the coconut oil in a large frying pan over medium–high heat. Add the mince, spices, garlic, onion, capsicum and tomato and cook, stirring occasionally to break up any lumps, for about 5 minutes, until the mince is cooked through and the tomato has broken down. Set aside and keep warm.

To make the tortillas, whisk together the flours, egg whites, lime zest and juice, sea salt and filtered water in a large bowl to form a smooth batter.

Heat 1 teaspoon of coconut oil in a large non-stick frying pan over low heat and pour 3 tablespoons of batter into the pan. Tilt and swirl the pan to spread the batter into a thin, round tortilla shape, about 12 cm in diameter. Turn the heat up to medium and cook for 2 minutes, or until light golden brown on the bottom, then carefully flip and cook for a further 1–2 minutes. Repeat this process, adding a little more oil each time, to make four tortillas.

To assemble, load up the tortillas with a good amount of the beef mince mixture. Spoon over some guacamole, add a generous drizzle of the lemon and paprika aioli and top with some rocket leaves and the egg halves. Now wrap up with your hands and get set to eat up a storm!

## TIP

Don't waste your yolks as they can be used for heaps of awesome recipes! From mayonnaise and aioli to custard and curds, be sure to always utilise your leftovers in some way.

While I'm a big fan of the classic Middle Eastern baked egg dish shakshuka, I've always thought it could be taken to the next level by beefing it up, literally! This vibrant breakfast dish is a great start to any day – just place the pan in the middle of the table for a fantastic centrepiece.

SERVES 2

# BEEFED-UP SHAKSHUKA

2 tablespoons coconut oil
2 garlic cloves, finely chopped
1 onion, finely chopped
1 long red chilli, deseeded and finely chopped
½ red capsicum, deseeded and finely diced
300 g beef mince
2 tablespoons chopped flat-leaf parsley leaves, plus 1 tablespoon extra, to serve
2 tablespoons chopped coriander leaves, plus 1 tablespoon extra to serve
2 tablespoons ground cumin
2 tablespoons smoked paprika
1 x 400 g can crushed tomatoes
4 eggs

Melt the coconut oil in a large frying pan over medium heat. Add the garlic, onion and chilli and cook for 2–3 minutes, or until softened, then add the capsicum and cook, stirring, for another 5 minutes, until lovely and soft.

Add the mince, herbs and spices and cook, stirring, until the meat is browned all over. Stir in the tomatoes and cook for 5–10 minutes, or until the sauce has thickened and the flavours are well combined.

Using the back of a wooden spoon, create four indentations in the sauce and crack an egg into each one, then cover the pan with a lid and cook for a further 5 minutes, until the whites are just cooked and the yolks are still a little soft. You may need to baste the whites with a little of the sauce as you go to ensure they cook properly.

To serve, finish with a sprinkling of chopped parsley and coriander and place in the centre of the table for everyone to dig in.

## TIP

Try mixing things up a little by using different types of mince. Lamb works wonderfully, as does chicken and pork. If you are looking to get ahead, you can make this up to the point where you add the eggs, then either chill or freeze the mixture until required.

When I want a sweet, slightly decadent start to my day I like to turn to this loaf. Inspired by traditional banana bread, the coconut and blueberries add an extra layer of flavour and are a great combo. Great fresh out of the oven on its own, this becomes truly epic when slathered with coconut cream and drizzled with honey.

MAKES 1 LOAF

# COCONUT AND BLUEBERRY LOAF WITH WHIPPED VANILLA COCONUT CREAM

250 g desiccated or shredded coconut

6 eggs

3 tablespoons maple syrup

1 vanilla pod, split and seeds scraped

1 teaspoon baking powder

1 large, very ripe banana, mashed

250 g (1½ cups) frozen blueberries

**To serve**

Whipped Vanilla Coconut Cream (page 211)

drizzle of honey

Get started by preheating the oven to 180°C and lining a 22 cm loaf tin with baking paper.

Put three-quarters of the coconut in a food processor and blitz until it forms a crumbly, flour-like consistency (be mindful not to over-process it though, as it will turn into coconut butter).

In a large bowl, beat the eggs, maple syrup, vanilla seeds and baking powder together by hand or with a hand mixer for 2–3 minutes, or until well combined. Add the mashed banana and stir to combine.

Fold the coconut flour into the egg mixture, then gently fold through three-quarters of the blueberries. Pour the batter into the prepared loaf tin, scatter over the rest of the blueberries and coconut and bake for 45 minutes, or until golden brown and cooked through. To test, press down gently on the top of the loaf – if it holds its shape, it's ready.

Remove the loaf from the oven, turn out of the tin and leave to cool slightly on a wire rack (if you're patient enough!), then slice and enjoy with a generous slather of whipped vanilla coconut cream and a drizzle of honey.

## TIP

I like to keep this loaf in an airtight container in the pantry or fridge, where it will last for up to 7 days. I then slice it and enjoy as before or grill it and spread generously with butter or coconut oil.

There's no better way of getting your daily dose of greens than in your morning slice of toast! This breakfast bread tastes incredible and packs a nutrient-dense punch, making it a fantastic substitute for traditional bread. If you have trouble convincing the kids to eat vegetables, well, here is your solution ...

MAKES 1 LOAF

# BROCCOLI BREAKFAST BREAD WITH PALEO COTTAGE CHEESE AND LEMON

½ head of broccoli, broken
  into florets
1 large zucchini
5 eggs
155 g (1½ cups) almond
  or hazelnut meal
1 tablespoon baking
  powder
pinch of sea salt
pinch of freshly ground
  black pepper
Paleo Cottage Cheese
  (page 259), to serve
lemon zest and juice,
  to serve

Preheat the oven to 180°C and line a 22 cm loaf tin with baking paper.

Place the broccoli, zucchini and eggs in a food processor and blend to a smooth puree. Pour the mixture into a large bowl, fold in the almond or hazelnut meal, baking powder, salt and pepper, and mix well to form a smooth, lump-free batter.

Pour the batter into the prepared loaf tin and bake for 45 minutes or until golden brown and cooked through. To test, press down gently on the top of the loaf – if it holds its shape, it's ready.

Remove the loaf from the oven and leave to sit in the tin for 5 minutes, then turn out onto a wire rack to cool completely. Enjoy straight away with some dollops of paleo cottage cheese, a sprinkling of lemon zest and a squeeze of lemon juice or, if eating later, toast under the grill for best results. To store, cover in plastic wrap or keep in an airtight container in the fridge for up to 5 days.

## TIP

Can't eat eggs? No problem! Soak 65 g of chia seeds in 250 ml (1 cup) of filtered water for about 10 minutes to form a gel and use this as a substitute.

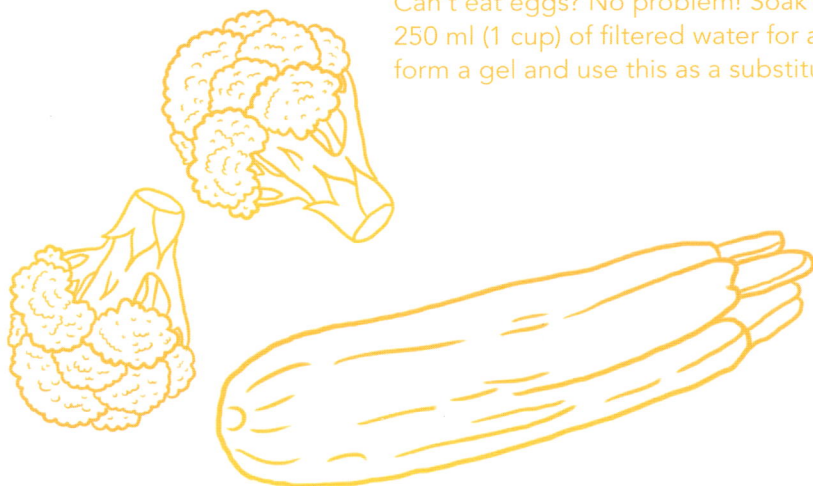

Broccoli breakfast bread, page 65

*Coconut and blueberry loaf, page 64*

COCONUT
YOGHURT

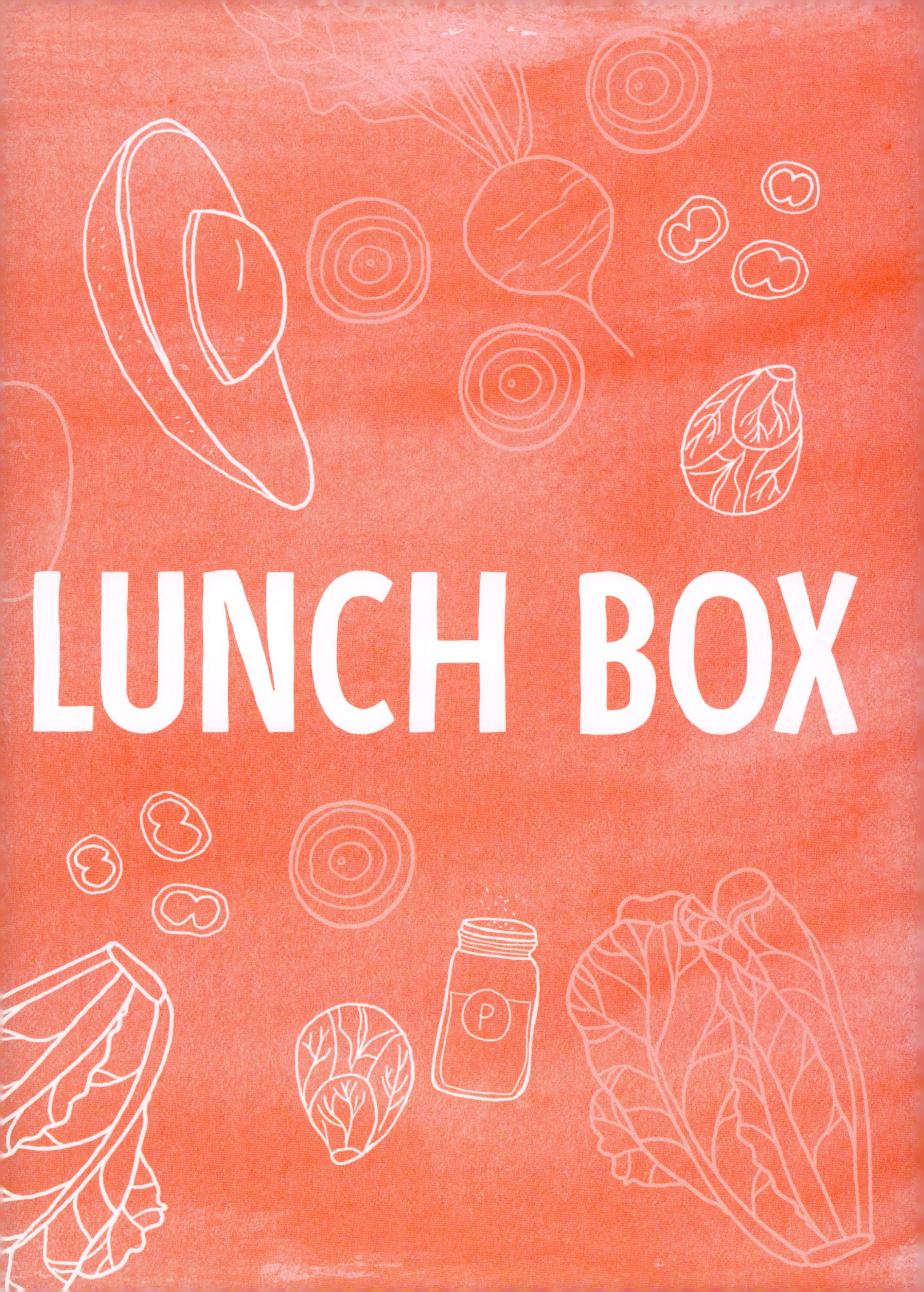

# LUNCH BOX

These delicious turmeric crackers are so easy to make. Don't be scared off by the length of the dehydrating time – other than turning them halfway through they don't require any attention and you can get on with other things while this is going on. Give them a go once and I promise you won't be buying store-bought crackers again!

SERVES 4

# TURMERIC SEED CRACKERS

170 g (1 cup) linseeds
3 tablespoons pumpkin seeds
3 tablespoons sunflower seeds
3 tablespoons sesame seeds
filtered water
½ teaspoon sea salt
½ tablespoon curry powder
2 teaspoons ground turmeric
1 teaspoon garlic powder

Place the linseeds, pumpkin seeds, sunflower seeds and sesame seeds in a bowl and cover with filtered water. Transfer to the fridge to soak overnight.

The next day, drain and rinse well, then combine the mixed seeds, salt, curry powder, turmeric and garlic powder in a food processor and pulse briefly to combine. (You want the seeds to break down slightly but not be completely ground, so be careful not to over-pulse.)

Preheat the oven to 50°C and line two baking trays with baking paper.

Spread the seed mix out on the lined baking trays in a very thin, even layer, then transfer to the oven and leave to dehydrate for 3 hours. Turn the sheets over carefully using a spatula, return to the oven and leave for another 3 hours, or until the seed sheets have dried out and are light golden and crisp.

Remove the seed sheets from the oven and allow to cool completely, then cut into squares with a knife or snap into shards. Store in an airtight container for up to 2 weeks.

## TIP

You can vary the flavours of the crackers by simply swapping the Indian-inspired curry powder and turmeric for Italian, Mexican or even Middle Eastern spices. Get creative guys! Also, feel free to switch the seeds for any of your other favourites.

This Middle Eastern-inspired dip is a big favourite of mine. Packed with flavour and with a deep purple-red colour that jumps off the plate, it's the perfect replacement for regular hummus for those who don't eat legumes. You can't help but feel vibrant after enjoying this!

SERVES 4

# BEETROOT 'HUMMUS'

3 beetroot (about 500 g)
90 g (⅓ cup) tahini
2 garlic cloves, finely chopped
2 tablespoons extra-virgin olive oil
zest and juice of 1 lemon
1 tablespoon apple cider vinegar
2 teaspoons ground cumin
½ teaspoon sea salt

Preheat the oven to 200°C.

Wrap the beetroot in foil, place on a baking tray and roast for 45 minutes, or until soft and tender (you can check by piercing the beetroot with a paring knife – if it goes through easily, they're cooked). Remove from the oven and set aside until cool enough to handle, then peel and roughly chop.

Add the beetroot to a food processor with the remaining ingredients and blend to a smooth puree. Store in an airtight container in the fridge for up to 5 days and enjoy with my seed crackers (opposite) or veggie dippers (see page 75).

## HEALTH BOOST

As well as being packed with essential nutrients, including manganese, potassium, iron and vitamin C, beetroot have also been proven to increase blood flow, which not only helps to transport nutrients around our body but also aids the detoxification process.

Turmeric seed crackers, page 70

Super simple spinach
and tahini dip, page 74

Beetroot 'hummus', page 71

Easy peasy veggie dippers, page 75

I can't get enough of this dip – it's the perfect combo of vibrant greens and delicious, creamy tahini. If you like yours a little zestier, just up the lemon!

SERVES 4

# SUPER SIMPLE SPINACH AND TAHINI DIP

1 tablespoon coconut oil
1 onion, diced
1 long red chilli, deseeded
   and finely chopped
4 garlic cloves, finely
   chopped
250 g baby spinach leaves
3 tablespoons filtered water
120 g tahini
100 ml extra-virgin olive oil
zest and juice of 2 lemons,
   plus extra if necessary
50 g (⅓ cup) macadamia
   nuts
sea salt and freshly ground
   black pepper

Melt the coconut oil in a large saucepan over medium heat. Add the onion and sauté for 4 minutes, or until soft and caramelised. Add the chilli and garlic and sauté for a further 4 minutes, until softened and aromatic, then add the spinach leaves and filtered water. Cover with a lid and simmer for 4 minutes, until nice and soft.

Remove the pan from the heat and set aside to cool slightly, then transfer the mixture to a food processor together with the tahini, olive oil, lemon zest and juice and macadamias. Season well with salt and pepper and whiz together until smooth.

Taste again and add a little more lemon juice and zest if you like, then enjoy with my turmeric seed crackers and veggie dippers (see page 70 and opposite). The dip will keep stored in an airtight container in the fridge for up to 5 days.

## HEALTH BOOST

The spinach makes this dip a good source of iron, while the tahini gives us a nice dose of B vitamins – great for everything from increased energy to helping deal with anxiety.

I love my veggie dippers, which are really just raw vegetables cut up into cute little portions for using in place of chips with dips. These are great for packing into school lunches and even better to have on hand when you're feeling peckish in the afternoon.

MAKES HOWEVER MUCH YOU CHOP UP!

# EASY PEASY VEGGIE DIPPERS

carrots
fennel
celery
cucumber
capsicum
cherry tomatoes
radishes

Possibly the easiest recipe in this book – just wash and chop up your chosen veg into your preferred serving size/shape. Now you're good to go!

## TIP

I like to pack away and freeze the carrot and capsicum dippers in freezer bags to ensure I always have a batch on hand. Give it a go – it's a fun task to do and will leave you feeling prepped like a boss.

I love this recipe because it's a great example of how easy it can be to create your own healthy muesli bars – perfect for school or work lunch boxes – at home. Like most of my recipes, you can play around and tweak the ingredients here to suit your personal taste, but this is an awesome starting point.

MAKES 10

# EPIC MUESLI BARS

155 g (1 cup) almonds, roughly chopped

80 g (½ cup) macadamia nuts or pecans roughly chopped

30 g (½ cup) shredded coconut

60 g (½ cup) dried blueberries

60 g (½ cup) pumpkin seeds

60 g (½ cup sunflower seeds

50 g (⅓ cup) sesame seeds

40 g (⅓ cup) chia seeds

1 tablespoon orange or lemon zest (optional)

125 ml (½ cup) maple syrup

3 tablespoons coconut oil, melted

Preheat the oven to 180°C. Grease and line a 35 cm x 25 cm baking tin with baking paper.

In a large bowl, mix together the nuts, coconut, blueberries, seeds and citrus zest (if using) until well combined. Stir in the maple syrup and coconut oil and mix well to coat everything evenly.

Pour the mixture into the prepared baking tin, levelling it out with the back of a wooden spoon. Bake for 15–20 minutes or until golden brown.

Remove the tray from the oven and leave to cool for 20 minutes or so, then gently lift the slab out of the tin using the baking paper. Transfer it to the fridge for another 30 minutes to firm up further. Cut into 10 slices, then wrap each individually in baking paper and tie with string (this will prevent the slices from sticking together). Store in the fridge for up to 10 days.

## TIP

Feel free to switch the macadamias and pecans here for any other types of nut you love. If you can't get hold of dried blueberries then raisins will work just fine, too.

School lunches SORTED!

# FAT
# IS YOUR
# FRIEND

For too many years, fat was demonised and stripped from our diets in the mistaken belief that 'fat makes us fat'. While this couldn't be further from the truth, the result of this war against fat was the rise of the low-fat food phenomenon, whereby for foods to still taste great after having all their natural fats extracted, a whole heap of extra sugar was added. This has led to the crises we are currently experiencing with the rise of obesity levels, type-2 diabetes and other weight- and sugar-related health problems. The fact of the matter is that good-quality sources of fat are your friends and should be celebrated as part of a healthy, balanced diet. Coconut products, nuts, seeds, animal fats from animals who have had a happy and natural life (and, very importantly, consumed a natural diet), not to mention avocados and olives all offer us wonderful sources of fat which can help boost our immune system and lose excess weight, assist in the absorption of nutrients, increase our metabolism and promote healthy hair, skin and nails. You've gotta be happy with fat … I mean that.

This is my healthy take on a hot pocket, for anyone who remembers them! The original was a microwaveable pastry pouch stuffed with all sorts of things from meat to cheese. My version is super healthy and delicious and can be stuffed with anything you like, including last night's leftovers, but I love this combo of crisp bacon, tender chicken pieces and sautéed veg. I recommend making this recipe the night before and enjoying it cold for lunch the next day.

SERVES 2

# CRISPY CHICKEN AND BACON SWEET POTATO POCKETS

80 ml (⅓ cup) coconut oil
2 small sweet potatoes, scrubbed
sea salt
1 garlic clove, very finely chopped
1 long red chilli, finely chopped
4 rindless bacon rashers, roughly chopped
1 x 180 g chicken breast fillet, diced
¼ head of broccoli, broken into small florets
¼ head of cauliflower, broken into small florets
1 handful of brussels sprouts, trimmed and finely sliced
2 large handfuls of baby spinach leaves
freshly ground black pepper
Paleo Sour Cream (see page 259), to serve

Get started by preheating the oven to 200°C and lining a baking tray with baking paper.

Rub 2 tablespoons of the coconut oil into the skin of the sweet potatoes and season generously with sea salt. Prick the sweet potatoes with a fork a couple of times, then place on the prepared tray and roast for 45 minutes. Remove the sweet potatoes from the oven and make a cut into each lengthways without cutting all the way through. Set aside.

Melt the remaining coconut oil in a large frying pan over medium heat. Add the garlic and chilli and sauté for 3–4 minutes, then add the bacon and sauté for 4–5 minutes, until starting to crisp. Add the diced chicken, broccoli, cauliflower and brussels sprouts and sauté for a further 5 minutes, or until the chicken is cooked through and the vegetables are soft. Stir in the baby spinach and cook for another minute to wilt slightly. Remove from the heat and season well with salt and pepper.

Scoop the chicken and bacon mixture into the sweet potato pockets and serve topped with a dollop of paleo sour cream, or store in an airtight container and enjoy cold for lunch the next day.

## HEALTH BOOST

For those wanting to eliminate grains, beans and legumes from their diet, sweet potato is a wonderful source of delicious slow-release energy, helping to prevent the blood-sugar spikes linked to fatigue and weight gain that can often result from eating carbohydrate-rich foods.

Kids love things wrapped up in lettuce cups and, being a big kid at heart, so do I! They're easy to hold, can be packed with whatever flavours you fancy and are so easy to prepare. These Thai chicken balls in lettuce cups make a fantastic lunch box filler whatever your age. Go on, give them a try – you really can't go wrong.

SERVES 6

# THAI CHICKEN BALLS IN LETTUCE CUPS

coconut oil, for greasing
400 g chicken thigh fillets
  or chicken mince
2 garlic cloves
zest and juice of 2 limes
85 ml coconut cream
2 tablespoons fish sauce
2 tablespoons chopped
  coriander leaves
1 long red chilli, deseeded
  and finely chopped
  (optional)

**To serve**
6 iceberg lettuce leaves
1 Lebanese cucumber,
  sliced
1 avocado, finely sliced
125 ml (½ cup) Paleo Sour
  Cream (see page 259)
1 tablespoon peanuts,
  toasted (optional)
lime wedges

Get started by preheating the oven to 180°C and generously greasing a large 6-hole muffin tin with coconut oil.

Place the chicken, garlic, lime zest and juice, coconut cream, fish sauce, coriander and chilli (if using) in a food processor and pulse until well combined.

Using your hands, divide the mixture into six equal-sized pieces and roll into balls. Place the meatballs in the greased muffin tin and bake for 15 minutes or until cooked through. Remove from the oven and set aside to cool slightly (if you're packing these up for school lunches, pop them in an airtight container and keep them in the fridge with the accompaniments until needed).

To serve, place a meatball in the centre of a lettuce cup along with some slices of cucumber and avocado. Top with a dollop of my paleo sour cream, a scattering of toasted peanuts, if you like, and lime wedges for squeezing over. Pick it up and dig in.

This is a GREAT example of a recipe that is EGG and NUT FREE, making it perfect for ANYONE with allergies.

This is the perfect recipe for those who spend a lot of time in the office! It requires minimal equipment and can be made on the fly with supermarket staples or any delicious leftovers you might have. Whatever you do though, just make sure you don't use your boss's favourite coffee mug to make it!

SERVES 1

# 2-MINUTE MEAL IN A MUG

coconut oil, for greasing
2 eggs
2 tablespoons almond milk
4 cherry tomatoes, quartered
¼ capsicum, deseeded and finely chopped
4 broccoli or cauliflower florets, very finely diced
4 black olives, pitted and finely chopped
100 g leftover roast chicken or veg (optional)

Grease a mug with a little coconut oil. Crack the eggs into a second mug, add the almond milk and whisk together with a fork.

Add the rest of the ingredients to the greased mug. Microwave on high for 60 seconds, then stir in the whisked egg and almond milk mixture and microwave for a further 30–60 seconds until the egg is set. Dig in.

## TIP

You can really add whatever leftovers you like to this, so get creative and mix things up a bit! No microwave? No worries. Simply pop all the ingredients in a ramekin and bake in an oven preheated to 180°C for 12 minutes.

This is my ode to *Gossip Girl*'s iconic Upper East Side character Blair Waldorf. In what way, you might ask? Well, the flavours of this classic salad are every bit as delicious to eat as she is to watch!

SERVES 2

# THE BLAIR WALDORF

250 g (1 cup) coconut
   yoghurt
2 celery stalks, 1 diced
   and 1 halved crossways,
   to serve
50 g (½ cup) walnut halves,
   toasted
1 pear, cored and diced
sea salt and freshly ground
   black pepper

Divide the coconut yoghurt, diced celery, walnuts and pear between two jars and season with salt and pepper. Store in the fridge and eat within 2 days of making, giving the jars a good shake before serving to mix everything together. Serve with the celery halves as dippers for scooping.

A Greek salad for any occasion! I love cooking up some lamb cutlets the night before and enjoying them cold as dippers with this salad jar.

SERVES 2

# GO GREEK

250 g (1 cup) coconut
   yoghurt
3 tablespoons finely
   chopped mint leaves
1 Lebanese cucumber,
   diced
10 kalamata olives, pitted
   and halved
¼ red onion, finely chopped
8 cherry tomatoes, halved
¼ green or yellow
   capsicum, deseeded
   and diced
2 tablespoons pine nuts,
   toasted
2 tablespoons extra-virgin
   olive oil
juice of 1 lemon
sea salt and freshly ground
   black pepper

In a bowl, combine the coconut yoghurt and mint leaves. Spoon this mixture into the bottom of two jars and top with the cucumber, olives, onion, tomato, capsicum and pine nuts. Drizzle over the extra-virgin olive oil, squeeze over the lemon juice and season with salt and pepper. Store in the fridge and eat within 2 days of making, giving the jars a good shake before serving to mix everything together.

Filled with the fresh, zesty flavours of Mexico, this epic little jar will make you the envy of your colleagues! Enjoy it simply as it is or – even better – with some leftover crunchy sweet potato skins (see page 100) for scooping.

SERVES 2

# MEXICAN MADNESS

250 ml (1 cup) Paleo Sour Cream (page 259)
1 avocado, cut into chunks
8 cherry tomatoes, halved
½ red capsicum, deseeded and roughly chopped
½ bunch of coriander, leaves picked and roughly torn
½ long red chilli, roughly chopped
¼ red onion, finely chopped
½ teaspoon ground cumin
sea salt and freshly ground black pepper

Divide the ingredients between two jars and season with salt and pepper. Store in the fridge and eat within 2 days of making, giving the jars a good shake before serving to mix everything together.

## TIP

As I like things nice and spicy, I like to use the whole chilli here, including the membrane and seeds. For a milder heat, scrape away the membrane and seeds with a sharp knife before chopping.

This salad jar is the perfect way to use up that leftover roast chook!

SERVES 2

# RIPPIN' ROAST CHICKEN

2 handfuls of baby spinach or rocket leaves
½ quantity Raw Apple Slaw (see page 114) or ½ carrot, grated
200 g shredded roast chicken
2 tablespoons Lemon and Smoked Paprika Aioli (see page 258)
½ avocado, diced
leftover Crunchy Sweet Potato Skins (see page 100), to serve

Divide the spinach or rocket between two jars and layer over the apple slaw or carrot, roast chicken, aioli and avocado. Store in the fridge and eat within 2 days of making, giving the jars a good shake before serving to mix everything together. Accompany with sweet potato skins for scooping.

## TIP

This little jar is super versatile. Made roast lamb or beef cheeks the night before? Use them here instead of the chicken. Not a fan of baby spinach leaves? Simply switch them out for your favourite green lettuce leaves instead. It's all good!

Rippin' roast chicken, page 87

Go Greek, page 86

The Blair Waldorf, page 86

Mexican madness, page 87

This is the ultimate veggie lunch! It's a great way to use up any veg you may have lurking in the fridge or experiment by adding new, delicious vegetables to your life.

SERVES 2

# RAINBOW CONNECTION

1 carrot

1 Lebanese cucumber, diced

½ fennel bulb, sliced into thin discs

¼ head of cauliflower, finely sliced

10 cherry tomatoes, halved

1 avocado, diced

1 handful of rocket or baby spinach leaves

3 tablespoons Go-to Salad Dressing or Green Goodness Dressing (see page 263)

Using a mandoline, spiraliser or a sharp knife, cut the carrot into fine vegetable noodles.

Divide the carrot noodles between two jars and layer over the cucumber, fennel, cauliflower, tomato, avocado and rocket or spinach leaves. Store in the fridge and eat within 2 days of making, adding your chosen dressing and giving the jars a good shake before serving to mix everything together.

## TIP

The veg I've suggested here is my all-time favourite combination, but I definitely like to mix it up with whatever I have in the house. I also like to play around with the shapes I cut the vegetables into to change up the textures. I encourage you to do the same – go on, make this recipe yours!

This is healthy fish and chips for work! Canned fish is a quick, easy and nutritious option – just make sure that the type you choose is sustainable and ethically sourced. Use leftover avocado fries that you've made for dinner the night before.

SERVES 1–2

# GONE FISH'N LUNCH BOX

200 g canned sardines, mackerel, tuna or salmon, broken into chunks

1 baby gem lettuce, leaves separated

leftover Awesome Avocado Fries (see page 97)

2 tablespoons Lemon and Smoked Paprika Aioli (see page 258)

Pack the ingredients up separately into a lunch box and keep in the fridge for up to 2 days. To serve, take a lettuce leaf and pile it up first with a chunk or two of fish, then top with an avocado fry or two and finally a dollop of aioli. Wrap it up and enjoy, then repeat!

These burgers are a fantastic option for work and school lunches. Because there's no meat in them, they're lunch-box safe on those warmer days, making them perfect for kids. I also love this Indian-inspired coconut and cucumber raita as it is so versatile – try serving it alongside a curry or using it to top fritters – it'll soon become one of your sure-fire favourites.

MAKES ABOUT 5

# INDIAN-SPICED QUINOA BURGER WITH COCONUT AND CUCUMBER RAITA

200 g (1 cup) red quinoa, rinsed

sea salt

1 zucchini, grated and squeezed to remove excess moisture

1 handful of coriander leaves

1 handful of mint leaves

2 eggs, whisked

100 g (1 cup) almond meal

½ teaspoon curry powder

½ teaspoon ground turmeric

freshly ground black pepper

1 tablespoon coconut oil

## Coconut and cucumber raita

2 x 270 ml cans coconut cream

1 Lebanese cucumber, deseeded and diced

4 tablespoons mint leaves, finely chopped

1 teaspoon chopped dill fronds

½ teaspoon smoked paprika

½ teaspoon ground cumin

zest and juice of 1 lemon

pinch of sea salt and freshly ground black pepper

For the raita, scoop the solid cream from the coconut cans into a bowl. Add the remaining ingredients and stir well to combine, adding a little of the clear coconut liquid from the cans to loosen it if need be (you can keep the rest for smoothies). It should be thick and chunky. Transfer to the fridge to chill for at least 1 hour (it will keep in an airtight container for up to 1 week).

Bring 300 ml of water to the boil in a medium–large saucepan with a lid. Add the quinoa and a generous pinch of salt. Return to the boil then immediately put the lid on, reduce the heat to the lowest setting possible and simmer gently for 15 minutes. During this time, do not stir or move the quinoa in any way.

Remove the pan from the heat and let stand, still with the lid on, for up to 5 minutes. Remove the lid, gently fluff up the grains with a fork and set aside to cool.

Place 1½ cups of the cooled quinoa in a large bowl (save the leftovers for a salad) and add the zucchini, coriander, mint, egg, almond meal, curry powder and turmeric. Season with salt and pepper, then mix well until everything is incorporated. Use your hands to shape into five even-sized patties.

Heat the coconut oil in a large frying pan over medium heat, add the patties and cook for 3–4 minutes on each side, until golden and crisp. Enjoy warm or refrigerate to pack for lunch the next day.

## HEALTH BOOST

Quinoa has a super-high protein content, making it a perfect nutrition source for vegetarians and vegans. It also has a very low glycemic load, which means it releases its energy slowly and helps you maintain steady blood-sugar levels.

PARSLEY
S

# GROWN & GATHERED

While I'm sure you're expecting me to say I first experienced pakora in India or at an Indian restaurant, I actually fell in love with this dish at my favourite L.A. restaurant! They serve a delicious gluten-free cauliflower pakora, which I eat nearly every day when I am over there. It's a great starter or side and also makes a wonderful sharing dish for parties.

SERVES 4

# CRISPY CAULI PAKORAS

1 head of cauliflower, cut into very small florets
125 ml (½ cup) coconut oil
sea salt

**Batter**
3 tablespoons coconut flour, plus extra if necessary
2 tablespoons arrowroot or tapioca flour
1 teaspoon chilli powder
1 teaspoon ground coriander
1 teaspoon ground cumin
1 teaspoon ground turmeric
generous pinch of sea salt
250 ml (1 cup) filtered water

To make the batter, place the flours, spices and salt in a large bowl and mix well. Pour over the water, whisking all the while to avoid lumps, to form a smooth, thick batter. (If the batter is looking too thin, add a little extra coconut flour.) Add the cauliflower florets and coat well using your hands.

Melt the coconut oil in a deep frying pan over medium–high heat until nice and hot. To see if the oil is hot enough, add a small battered floret as a test – if it sizzles straight away, you're good to go!

Fry the battered florets in small batches for 4–5 minutes, until nicely browned, lowering them into the hot oil one at a time, spacing them out and being careful not to overcrowd the pan. Remove the cooked pakora from the pan using a slotted spoon and set aside on paper towel to drain, then repeat with the remaining florets (don't freak out if some of the batter sticks to the pan or comes off – this is normal).

Serve warm with a generous pinch or two of salt. These also taste amazing dipped into my coconut and cucumber raita (see page 92).

If you'd asked me six months ago for my view on hot avocado, I would have said 'NO, NO, *NO!*'. But that was before I experimented in the kitchen with these fries and fell in love with their crunchy outsides and beautiful soft insides. Now I'm sold on it – I hope you give this a try and become the same!

SERVES 4–6

# AWESOME AVOCADO FRIES

60 g (½ cup) arrowroot or tapioca flour

80 ml (⅓ cup) filtered water

50 g (½ cup) quinoa flakes

3 tablespoons black sesame seeds

3 tablespoons white sesame seeds

2 tablespoons chia seeds

1 tablespoon sweet paprika

2 teaspoons ground cumin

sea salt

2 avocados, cut into 2 cm thick wedges

3 tablespoons coconut oil

lemon wedges, to serve

Lemon and Smoked Paprika Aioli (see page 258), to serve (optional)

Whisk together the flour and filtered water in a bowl to form a thick batter.

In a separate bowl, add the quinoa flakes, sesame seeds, chia seeds, paprika, cumin and a generous pinch of salt and mix well to combine.

Dip the avocado slices into the batter, then coat with the sesame seed mixture, patting off any excess.

Heat the coconut oil in a frying pan over medium–high heat. To test the temperature, drop a small piece of avocado in the oil – if it bubbles instantly around the edges you are ready to go! Taking your time and working in batches, fry the avocado slices for about 1–2 minutes on each side, using tongs to turn them carefully, until the seedy coating is brown and crisp. Set aside on paper towel to drain.

Season with another generous pinch of salt and serve with lemon wedges for squeezing and lemon and smoked paprika aioli for dipping, if you like. Now devour!

Crunchy sweet potato skins with creamy zucchini, page 100

Awesome avocado fries, page 97

Crispy cauli pakoras, page 96

Brussels sprout dippers, page 101

This book is all about minimising time and waste in the kitchen, so I hope you love this double use of the humble sweet potato – if you've baked up some sweet potatoes to make into mash, puree or gnocchi, this is a great way of using up the skins that will be left over. Try swapping out the Italian herbs for whatever seasoning you like. Check out my seasonings on pages 264–265 for other creative ideas!

SERVES 4

# CRUNCHY SWEET POTATO SKINS WITH CREAMY ZUCCHINI

3 tablespoons coconut oil
skins from 5 baked sweet
    potatoes, torn into corn-
    chip-sized pieces
sea salt
1 teaspoon finely chopped
    rosemary or thyme leaves

**Creamy zucchini**
2 zucchini
3 tablespoons coconut oil
    or butter
2 garlic cloves, finely diced
sea salt and freshly ground
    black pepper

To make the creamy zucchini, coarsely grate the zucchini by hand or put them in a food processor with the grater attachment added. Wrap the grated zucchini in a tea towel and squeeze over a sink to remove as much excess liquid as possible.

Melt the coconut oil or butter in a frying pan over medium heat, add the garlic and sauté for 3 minutes, or until softened and slightly caramelised. Add the zucchini and cook, stirring, for 10 minutes, or until lovely and soft. Remove from the heat, season with salt and pepper and set aside to cool. Transfer to an airtight container and store in the fridge until needed (it will keep for 2–3 days). For an ever creamier consistency, you can blend the zucchini until smooth.

Melt the coconut oil in a deep frying pan over medium–high heat. To test if it is hot enough, simply drop a small piece of sweet potato skin into the oil – if it sizzles and bubbles you're good to go. Working in batches, add the sweet potato skins to the pan and fry for 1–3 minutes, turning with tongs, until golden brown and crisp on all sides. Remove from the pan and set aside on paper towel to drain and cool slightly, then season with a generous pinch of salt. Scatter over the chopped herbs and serve warm with the creamy zucchini on the side.

## TIPS

The creamy zucchini can be used for so many different things – try spreading it over seed crackers, on a slice of one of my breads or on a steak as a delicious topping. If you'd rather bake the sweet potato skins than fry them, simply toss them with 1 tablespoon of melted coconut oil and bake them in a 220°C preheated oven for 15–20 minutes, until golden brown and crisp.

Sautéed brussels sprouts are one of my all-time favourite side dishes, but recently I've put a new spin on them by dunking these delicious, crispy bundles of goodness into some of my tastiest dips and sauces. I think they make fantastic dippers but don't take my word for it – give them a go and see for yourself!

SERVES 4

# BRUSSELS SPROUT DIPPERS

125 ml (½ cup) coconut oil
500 g brussels sprouts, trimmed and halved
6 garlic cloves, finely sliced
sea salt
zest of 1 lemon
1 tablespoon chilli flakes (optional)
your choice of my Chimichurri, Chilli Macadamia Pesto, Lemon and Smoked Paprika Aioli or Less-Than-A-Minute Mayo (see pages 142, 255, 258 and 260), to serve

Melt the coconut oil in a large, heavy-based frying pan over medium heat. Add the brussels sprouts and garlic and shallow-fry for 5–6 minutes, or until golden brown and crisp on the outsides but still nice and crunchy.

Season generously with salt and sprinkle with the lemon zest and chilli flakes (if you like things hot), then get dunking into your dip of choice. These are best served warm straight out of the pan.

## HEALTH BOOST

Despite containing loads of fibre, vitamin C and protein, brussels sprouts often get a bad rap for being a bit smelly when cooking. Thankfully, this less-than-ideal odour is only released when you overcook them, which won't be a problem here! Plus, by making sure they aren't overdone, you help to retain all those epic nutrients that can otherwise be lost during the cooking process.

In case you hadn't already guessed I'm a huge fan of zucchini, and there are few better ways of enjoying them than these crispy, moreish chips – especially when dipped in my lemon and smoked paprika aioli. Kids and grown-ups alike go mad for these little tasties. They make the perfect accompaniment to my Chicken and macadamia burgers on page 138 – you wont be disappointed!

SERVES 4

# ZUCCHINI CHIPS WITH AIOLI

4 eggs
60 g (½ cup) arrowroot or
    tapioca flour
100 g (1 cup) almond meal
sea salt
1 teaspoon sweet paprika
½ teaspoon garlic powder
½ teaspoon ground cumin
2 large zucchini, cut into
    1 cm thick batons
coconut oil, for deep-frying
freshly ground black
    pepper
2 tablespoons finely
    chopped flat-leaf parsley,
    to serve
Lemon and Smoked Paprika
    Aioli (see page 258),
    to serve

Whisk the eggs in a bowl and place the flour in another bowl. In a third bowl, mix together the almond meal, 1 teaspoon of salt, the paprika, garlic powder and cumin.

Dip the zucchini batons first into the flour to coat, shaking off any excess, then into the egg mixture and finally into the seasoned almond meal mixture to coat.

Half-fill a heavy-based saucepan with coconut oil and set over medium heat. Heat the oil to 180°C. To test if it is hot enough, simply drop a small piece of zucchini into the oil – if it sizzles and bubbles you're good to go.

Carefully lower the zucchini pieces into the hot oil in small batches and cook for 2–4 minutes, until golden brown and crisp on all sides. Remove from the pan using metal tongs or a slotted spoon and transfer to paper towel to drain. Repeat with the remaining zucchini, then season with salt and pepper. Transfer to a serving plate, scatter over the parsley and serve with the lemon and smoked paprika aioli.

This tray of roast vegetables is perfect for when you're pressed for time putting dinner together but still crave the fantastic flavours and nutrients that only a plate of fresh veggies can deliver. There's just one tray, it's easy to prepare and tastes super delicious! I like it nice and simple, but you can always trick it up by finishing it off with some toasted seeds or nuts, or by spooning over a little aioli or pesto, if you like. Go on, make it yours!

SERVES 2

# MY LITTLE TRAY OF DELICIOUSNESS

½ red cabbage, outer leaves removed, roughly shredded

100 g brussels sprouts, trimmed and quartered

2 fennel bulbs, sliced into discs

2 tablespoons coconut oil, melted

2 tablespoons Texan Seasoning (see page 265)

Get started by preheating the oven to 200°C and lining a baking tray with baking paper.

In a bowl, generously coat the prepared vegetables in the coconut oil and seasoning. Arrange the veg over the prepared baking tray in an even layer and bake for 30 minutes, or until golden brown around the edges and soft in the middle. Divide between plates and serve.

## TIP

I love to double the quantities here and pop an extra tray in the oven when I make this, so that I have loads of lovely roasted veggies for next day's lunch, saving me time in the kitchen later. Too easy.

I love roasted carrots and pumpkin, and the addition of this super-easy herb and garlic glaze together with the dukkah coating takes them to the next level! Sometimes the simplest meals are the best.

SERVES 4

# HERB-GLAZED ROASTED CARROTS AND PUMPKIN WITH DUKKAH

4 carrots, halved lengthways
200 g pumpkin, peeled and cut into chunky squares
1 x quantity Macadamia Dukkah (see page 264)

### Glaze

4 rosemary sprigs, leaves picked
4 thyme sprigs, leaves picked
4 garlic cloves
1 tablespoon coconut oil, melted
1 tablespoon coconut aminos
generous pinch of sea salt and freshly ground black pepper

Preheat the oven to 200°C and line a baking tray with baking paper.

To make the glaze, pound the herbs, garlic, coconut oil and coconut aminos in a mortar and pestle or whiz together in a food processor to form a lovely, smooth paste. Season with salt and pepper.

Coat the vegetable pieces generously with the glaze, then arrange on the prepared baking tray and bake for 45 minutes, or until golden brown and cooked through. Remove from the oven and sprinkle over the dukkah to coat evenly. To serve, take the baking tray to the table for that rustic feel.

### TIP

Wondering what I mean when I refer to coconut aminos? Well, it's a delicious and healthy sauce made from coconut sap. Sort of salty and slightly sweet in flavour, it resembles a light soy sauce but it is soy and gluten free, making it the perfect replacement for those following a paleo or clean-living lifestyle. It is available from most well-stocked health-food stores.

Frittata is SO versatile and DELICIOUS, you can eat it for breakfast, lunch or dinner.

I love this recipe and tend to cook it at least a couple of times a week. It's a complete meal in itself, and you can pretty much pack it with whatever you want! Choose to keep it simple or fill it with whatever leftovers you have in the fridge or freezer – it's all good …

SERVES 4

# FEED ME NOW FRITTATA

2 tablespoons coconut oil
2 garlic cloves, finely chopped
1 large onion, sliced
1 long red chilli, deseeded and finely chopped
2 zucchini, grated and squeezed to remove excess moisture
2 tablespoons chopped flat-leaf parsley leaves
sea salt and freshly ground black pepper
10 eggs
125 ml (½ cup) coconut cream

**Filling**

400 g leftover roast chicken or roast vegetables (see page 103), cut into small chunks

Get started by preheating the oven to 180°C.

Melt the coconut oil in an ovenproof frying pan over medium heat and sauté the garlic, onion and chilli until softened and slightly caramelised, about 3–5 minutes. Add the grated zucchini, parsley and your choice of lovely filling and sauté for another 4 minutes or so until softened. Season with salt and pepper.

In a bowl, whisk together the eggs and coconut cream until smooth and creamy. Pour this over the filling mixture in the pan, then bake in the oven for 20–30 minutes, or until the frittata is golden on top and the egg is cooked through.

Leave to cool in the pan for at least 10 minutes, then cut into portions and serve.

## TIP

I love making this recipe in advance for the week ahead. It's perfect enjoyed cold with a fresh salad for lunch or warmed up for dinner on a busy weeknight when you haven't time to get in the kitchen properly.

There is something so incredibly nourishing about a simple plate of fresh greens, and that's why I really wanted to include this recipe: to showcase how easy it is to get your daily dose of these beauties in such a flavoursome way!

SERVES 4 AS A SIDE

# SAUTÉED GREENS WITH LEMON AND GARLIC

1 bunch of broccolini
1 large bunch of asparagus, trimmed
2 tablespoons coconut oil
2 garlic cloves, sliced
1 long red chilli, finely sliced
2 zucchini, sliced lengthways into thin strips
¼ bunch of kale, stalks removed and leaves coarsely chopped
zest and juice of 2 lemons
2 tablespoons extra-virgin olive oil
2 tablespoons slivered almonds, toasted, to serve
sea salt and freshly ground black pepper

Blanch the broccolini and asparagus in a large saucepan of boiling water for 2–3 minutes, until just tender. Drain and set aside.

Melt the coconut oil in a large frying pan over medium heat. Add the garlic and chilli and sauté for about 4 minutes, until softened and fragrant, then add the zucchini, kale and the blanched vegetables, and sauté for a further 4 minutes, or until the zucchini has softened and the kale has wilted.

Pile the veg onto a serving platter, drizzle over the lemon juice and extra-virgin olive oil and scatter over the lemon zest and toasted almonds. Season with salt and pepper and serve.

## TIP

These greens are also lovely with some of my Turmeric and tahini dressing (see page 262) drizzled over them.

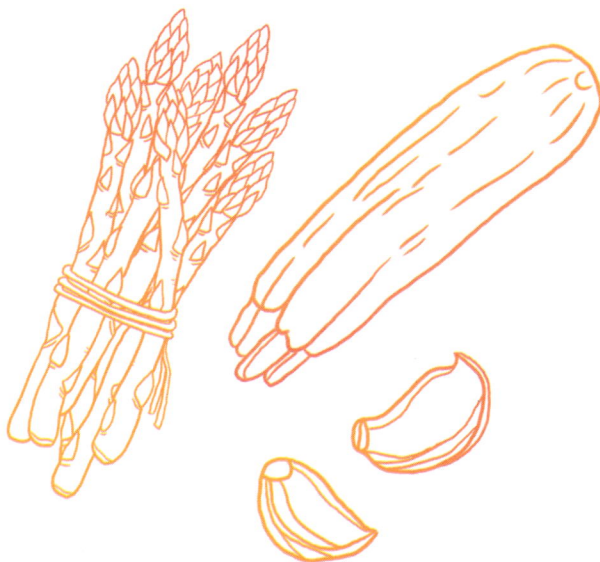

# YOU CAN DO IT

When transitioning to a healthier lifestyle, you will have ups and you will have downs, but the key is to always remind yourself that you've got it covered, no matter how hard it seems. I want you to believe in yourself and know you can do this. There's always a new day ahead, something that's incredibly exciting as it brings another opportunity to learn, grow and evolve in this life. It is all about making small, daily incremental steps that lead to sustainable, enjoyable life-long habits that you actually love. There's no quick fix or magic pill, and no one can do it for you. Instead it is about backing yourself, stepping up and doing your best, without fear, guilt or judgement of yourself or others. On your journey there's no such thing as a step backwards, just the occasional side step – but the key is being present throughout everything, so you can learn from it all along the way. And once you have followed this way of life for a while incredible things start to happen. Waking up, the days seem brighter, life seems easier and you'll feel happier. It might take a week, a month or even a year, but someone close to you will come up to you and notice your eyes are brighter, your skin is clear and your whole body is full of life. They'll ask, 'what's your secret?'. And you can proudly say, 'I made healthy easy'.

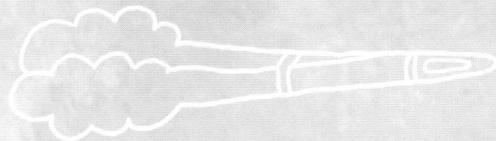

The bromance between cauliflower and broccoli here is a love story destined to end in deliciousness! I love roasting these two yummy cruciferous vegetables, as it really brings out their flavour and lovely, crunchy texture. This tastes great with seafood.

SERVES 4 AS A SIDE

# ROASTED BRAULIFLOWER

1 head of broccoli, broken into small florets
1 head of cauliflower, broken into small florets
80 ml (⅓ cup) coconut oil
6 garlic cloves, roughly chopped
sea salt and freshly ground black pepper
zest and juice of 1 lemon, to serve (optional)

Get started by preheating the oven to 200°C and lining two baking trays with baking paper.

Put the broccoli and cauliflower florets in a large bowl together with the coconut oil and garlic and mix well. Season with salt and pepper, then arrange on the prepared baking trays in an even layer (you don't want the broccoli and cauliflower to overlap as they won't crisp up as nicely). Roast in the oven for 30–45 minutes, moving everything around once or twice while cooking, until crisp and crunchy on the outside.

Pile into a serving bowl and top with the lemon zest and juice (if using). Season with salt and pepper and enjoy!

## TIP

To give this a bit of a meaty flavour boost, cut four rindless bacon rashers into bite-sized pieces, add to the bowl with the vegetables and cook as instructed.

Full of crunchy texture and bright flavours, this raw apple slaw is a great option for a light lunch or simple dinner. While it makes a fantastic meal in itself, it is also easy to pimp up by adding some extra protein – try stirring through some poached salmon or leftover roast chicken if you fancy something a bit more filling.

SERVES 4

# RAW APPLE SLAW

2 carrots, cut into matchsticks
2 beetroot, cut into matchsticks
2 green apples, cut into matchsticks or thin discs
½ fennel bulb, finely sliced
¼ red cabbage, outer leaves removed, shredded
2 large handfuls of mint leaves, shredded
2 handfuls of flat-leaf parsley leaves, roughly chopped
zest and juice of 2 lemons
3 tablespoons Lemon and Smoked Paprika Aioli (see page 258)
sea salt and freshly ground black pepper

Place the carrot, beetroot, apple, fennel and red cabbage in a large bowl, cover with cold water and set aside in the fridge for at least 30 minutes to soak (the longer you leave them, the crunchier and fresher they will taste).

When ready to serve, drain the ingredients and pat them dry with paper towel. Transfer to another large bowl, add the remaining ingredients and mix together well. Pile into a serving bowl, season with salt and pepper and enjoy. Any leftovers can be kept in an airtight container in the fridge for up to 5 days.

## HEALTH BOOST

Apples are packed with fibre and nutrients, including potassium, calcium, iron and vitamin C. Due to their sugar content, some people are wary of fruit like apples, but when enjoyed like this (and not processed into juices, for example), they make a wonderful addition to your plate.

I love a good gluten-free pizza, especially when it's topped with epic veg like this! I like incorporating it into my week as part of a 'meat-free Monday', but if you feel you really need a protein hit then you can always top it with some flaked poached fish, leftover cooked mince or grilled chicken. It's all good!

SERVES 4

# VEG LOVERS' PIZZA

1 head of cauliflower, florets and stalk roughly chopped
1 garlic clove, grated
½ onion, grated
pinch of sea salt
4 eggs
250 g (2½ cups) almond meal, plus extra if needed
1 zucchini, cut lengthways into very thin strips
1 carrot, cut lengthways into very thin strips
½ fennel bulb, sliced into very thin discs
2 tablespoons coconut oil, melted
4 tablespoons Garlicky No-tomato Pasta Sauce (see page 254)
4 roma tomatoes, sliced
2 tablespoons Cashew Feta (see page 261)
8 basil leaves, torn
1 tablespoon capers, rinsed
2 tablespoons Chilli Macadamia Pesto (see page 255)
1 tablespoon extra-virgin olive oil

Preheat the oven to 220°C and line a baking tray or pizza tray with baking paper.

Place the cauliflower, garlic, onion and salt in a food processor and whiz down to nice, rice-sized pieces. Tip the cauliflower into a bowl with the eggs and almond meal, and stir well to combine. The mixture should be dough-like in consistency – if it's looking a little crumbly, simply add some more almond meal until it holds together well.

Spread out the cauliflower 'dough' to a thickness of 15–20 mm in whatever shape you like, then bake for 15 minutes, or until it is lightly golden. Remove from the oven and reduce the temperature to 180°C.

Meanwhile, brush the zucchini, carrot and fennel pieces with the melted coconut oil, transfer them to a hot chargrill pan or barbecue and cook for 2–3 minutes on each side until golden brown and caramelised.

Cover the pizza base with the no-tomato sauce, layer over the sliced tomato and dot with the cashew feta. Bake for 10 minutes, or until the edges of the base are golden brown and the ingredients are cooked through. Remove from the oven and top with the zucchini and carrot strips, fennel, basil leaves, capers and dollops of the macadamia pesto. Drizzle over the olive oil and serve.

## HEALTH BOOST

Fennel is a good source of vitamin B6, which plays a vital role in breaking down carbohydrates and proteins into glucose and amino acids, meaning it's more easily utilised by the body for energy.

Quick, simple and delicious, this gluten-free vegan pasta is a fantastic dinner, and the leftovers are perfect for taking to work the next day! Sautéing the sweet potato noodles here helps to bring out their natural flavour and delivers a lovely texture just like *al dente* pasta.

SERVES 2

# VEGAN SWEET POTATO SPAGHETTI WITH MACADAMIA PESTO

1 large sweet potato
   (about 400 g)
2 tablespoons coconut oil
   (optional)
65 g (½ cup) Chilli
   Macadamia Pesto
   (see page 255)
4 macadamia nuts
basil leaves, to serve

Using a mandoline, spiraliser or a sharp knife, cut the sweet potato into fine noodles.

If you want to sauté the noodles, heat the coconut oil in a large frying pan over medium heat, add the sweet potato noodles and sauté for 8–10 minutes, until soft and golden brown. Alternatively, add the sweet potatoes to a pan of salted boiling water and cook for 5 minutes, or until tender, then drain and return to the pan.

Stir the pesto through the noodles to coat evenly, then divide between serving plates. Grate the macadamia nuts over the top of your dish – it will look just like parmesan – and garnish with a few basil leaves.

## TIP

If you want a protein boost you can always add a little lean meat to this – chicken works particularly well.

Whenever I travel to the States, I am always reminded of their love of mac 'n' cheese and how it forms a key part of their food culture. Although less common here in Australia, I'm certain that if I ate cheese or pasta I'd be a huge fan of the stuff! As it is, here's my vegetarian take on this North American favourite.

SERVES 4

# PALEO MAC 'N' CHEESE

### The 'cheese'

2 tablespoons coconut oil
   or butter
1 yellow zucchini or 100 g
   pattypan squash, cut
   into cubes
1 carrot, peeled and
   finely diced
½ red onion, diced
1 garlic clove, finely
   chopped
½ teaspoon dijon mustard
sea salt
250 ml (1 cup) coconut
   cream
1 egg yolk
freshly ground black
   pepper
grated macadamia nuts,
   to serve

### The 'mac'

2 tablespoons coconut oil
   or butter
1–2 heads of cauliflower,
   broken into small florets
½ teaspoon sea salt
3 tablespoons filtered water

To make the 'cheese', melt the coconut oil or butter in a heavy-based saucepan over medium heat. Add the zucchini, carrot, onion, garlic, mustard and ½ teaspoon of salt and sauté for 5–10 minutes, until the veg have started to soften and the onion is translucent. Pour over the coconut cream, bring to a simmer and cook for 5 minutes, then cover with a lid and cook for a further 5 minutes until the veg are nice and soft. Remove from the heat and set aside to cool slightly.

Meanwhile, make the 'mac'. Melt the coconut oil or butter in a large frying pan over high heat, add the cauliflower florets and salt and sauté for 4 minutes, or until lightly charred on all sides. Add the filtered water and cook for a further 4 minutes, stirring, until the cauliflower has softened and the water has evaporated. Remove from the heat, cover with a lid and set aside.

Transfer the cooled 'cheese' mixture to a food processor or blender and puree until nice and smooth. Add the egg yolk and whiz together well – the egg will thicken the sauce and give it a rich texture. Season to taste with salt and pepper. Transfer the cauliflower to a serving plate and pour over the 'cheese'. Sprinkle over a few grated macadamias and enjoy!

## TIP

Don't have any cauliflower on hand? That's cool; it may not look like the typical pasta version, but broccoli is also awesome in this dish!

# 30-MINUTE MEALS

There is no better go-to dish on a busy weeknight than fritters. You can utilise pretty much whatever vegetables you've got in the fridge and add any combination of herbs and spices. On this page and the following pages are some of my all-time favourites, starting with these delicious carrot and fennel fritters.

SERVES 2

# CARROT AND FENNEL FRITTERS

2 carrots, coarsely grated
1 fennel bulb, coarsely
    grated
¼ red onion, grated
55 g (½ cup) almond meal
1 tablespoon chilli flakes
sea salt
2 eggs
2 tablespoons coconut oil
freshly ground black
    pepper

**To serve**
lemon wedges
your favourite mixed leaves
Macadamia Ricotta (see
    page 261)
extra-virgin olive oil

In a bowl, combine the carrot, fennel, red onion, almond meal, chilli flakes, a pinch of salt and eggs to form a nice, thick batter.

Melt the coconut oil in a large frying pan over medium heat. Spoon the carrot and fennel batter mixture into the pan in four loose rounds and press down lightly on each to form round fritters. Cook for 2–3 minutes on each side, until cooked through and golden and crunchy on the outside.

Season with salt and pepper and serve with lemon wedges, your favourite mixed leaves, a good dollop of macadamia ricotta and a drizzle of extra-virgin olive oil.

Crispy PERFECTION on a plate!

I'm really loving the flavours of India at the moment, something this super-tasty fritter recipe reflects. These sweet potato fritters are as phenomenal to eat as they are simple to prepare – try serving them up with my coconut and cucumber raita to take them to the next level.

SERVES 2

# TURMERIC AND SWEET POTATO FRITTERS

1 large sweet potato, coarsely grated
¼ red onion, grated
55 g (½ cup) almond meal
1 tablespoon chilli flakes
2 tablespoons finely chopped coriander leaves
2 teaspoons ground turmeric
2 teaspoons ground cumin
sea salt
2 eggs
2 tablespoons coconut oil
freshly ground black pepper
lemon wedges, to serve
coconut and cucumber raita (see page 92), to serve (optional)

In a bowl, combine the sweet potato, red onion, almond meal, chilli flakes, coriander, turmeric, cumin, a pinch of salt and eggs to form a nice, thick batter.

Melt the coconut oil in a large frying pan over medium heat. Spoon the sweet potato batter mixture into the pan in four loose rounds and press down lightly on each to form round fritters. Cook for 2–3 minutes on each side, until cooked through and golden and crunchy on the outside.

Season with salt and pepper and serve with lemon wedges for squeezing and dollops of my coconut and cucumber raita, if you like.

This recipe is a great way to turn two of my favourite ingredients – cauliflower and broccoli – into the stars of your weeknight meal. Go on, give it a try. I promise that once you go flat, you'll never go back!

SERVES 2

# CAULIFLOWER AND BROCCOLI FRITTERS

½ head of broccoli, coarsely grated or blitzed
½ head of cauliflower, coarsely grated or blitzed
¼ red onion, grated
55 g (½ cup) almond meal
1 teaspoon smoked paprika
1 teaspoon ground coriander
1 teaspoon ground cumin
1 teaspoon chilli flakes
sea salt
2 eggs
2 tablespoons coconut oil
freshly ground black pepper
lemon wedges, to serve

In a bowl, combine the broccoli, cauliflower, red onion, almond meal, paprika, coriander, cumin, chilli flakes, a pinch of salt and the eggs to form a nice, thick batter.

Melt the coconut oil in a large frying pan over medium heat. Spoon the cauliflower and broccoli batter mixture into the pan in four loose rounds and press down lightly on each to form round fritters. Cook for 2–3 minutes on each side, until cooked through and golden and crunchy on the outside.

Season with salt and pepper and serve with lemon wedges for squeezing.

Short on time and got some leftover veggies in the crisper? Well then, look no further than this fantastic 4-minute noodle dish. It's versatile enough to have a protein stirred through it, but flavoursome enough to be a stand-alone meal in its own right.

SERVES 4

# 4-MINUTE NOODLES

2 zucchini
2 tablespoons coconut oil
½ onion, finely chopped
2 garlic cloves, finely
   chopped
1 long red chilli, deseeded
   and finely chopped
12 cherry tomatoes, halved
   (or 2 regular tomatoes,
   diced)
12 kalamata olives, pitted
   and halved
sea salt and freshly ground
   black pepper
2 tablespoons pine nuts,
   toasted
zest and juice of 1 lemon

Using a mandoline or sharp knife, cut the zucchini into thin strips, then cut each strip lengthways into noodle-sized pieces.

Heat the coconut oil in a large frying pan over medium heat. Add the onion, garlic and chilli and sauté for 2 minutes, or until the onion is translucent and everything is nicely aromatic. Add the cherry tomatoes and olives and cook, stirring gently, for a further 2 minutes, or until the tomato has softened.

Add the zucchini noodles to the pan and stir gently to coat them in all the lovely flavours, then season with salt and pepper to taste. Divide among four bowls and serve topped with the toasted pine nuts, a little lemon zest and a squeeze of lemon juice.

### TIP

Don't have a zucchini to hand? That's cool! You can make the noodles out of all sorts of other veg, such as carrots, pattypan squash and parsnip – they'll all taste just as awesome.

# GO WITH YOUR GUT HEALTH

There's a famous South American proverb that says 'good broth will resurrect the dead', and I'd have to say it's not far off the mark! If your grandma ever made you a traditional chicken soup as a kid, you can probably relate to it, too – all that lovely slow-cooking helps break down the multitudes of minerals and amino acids in the chicken bones and meat that normally wouldn't be so easy to digest, meaning your body can get the maximum amount of goodness out of every mouthful. In a similar way, the probiotics contained in fermented foods, such as sauerkraut, help to promote good bacteria in your gut, leading to improved digestion and absorption of all the foods you put inside your body. Also, both broths and fermented foods have been proven to support not just the body but also the mind, with research showing a direct correlation between repairing the gut and improved mental health. And finally, as many illnesses are born in the gut, once you heal and seal your gut lining with broths and ferments and help your digestive system start working properly, you'll be surprised by how many little issues and problems with your body start clearing up – there's a reason these foods have been eaten for thousands of years!

I absolutely *love* omelettes for dinner! They're a really quick way to give your body an abundance of nutrients together with a high-quality protein hit. Did you know eggs are referred to as complete proteins, meaning they contain all nine essential amino acids? These are the ones your body can't make and that we have to get from our food. This meal is sounding better already, huh!?

SERVES 1

# THE ULTIMATE DINNER OMELETTE WITH ROASTED ASPARAGUS

½ bunch of asparagus, trimmed
3 tablespoons coconut oil, melted
sea salt and freshly ground black pepper
3 eggs
3 tablespoons canned coconut milk
pinch of dried chilli flakes
1 handful of baby kale or rocket leaves
slice of my Broccoli Breakfast Bread (see page 65)

Get started by preheating the oven to 180°C and lining a baking tray with baking paper.

Coat the asparagus in 1 tablespoon of the coconut oil and season well with salt and pepper. Arrange on the baking tray in an even layer and roast in the oven for 8–10 minutes, until golden brown and tender. Set aside.

Meanwhile, in a bowl, whisk together the eggs and coconut milk until smooth, aerated and creamy.

Heat the remaining coconut oil in a frying pan over medium heat. Add the egg mixture and, using a rubber spatula, stir gently, while tilting the pan and moving it back and forth over the heat at the same time. (This keeps the egg from sticking or browning.)

As soon as the mixture changes from runny to thick and custardy, stop stirring. Season the omelette with salt and pepper and sprinkle over the chilli flakes, then, using a spatula, gently fold it in half. Serve immediately alongside the roasted asparagus, a handful of green leaves and a slice of my breakfast bread.

## TIP

Got leftovers? Then get pimping that omelette! Stuff it with whatever you've got hiding at the back of the fridge – think mince, beef cheeks … or even Nan's stew! While this omelette is at its best fresh, you can always make double and enjoy one cold for lunch the next day.

I have long been a fan of chicken schnitzels. Their crunchy, salty exteriors and soft juicy insides tick a lot of boxes for me. Another box they tick is the one marked 'quick and easy'. To tick the last box marked 'healthy', I've given them one hell of a makeover here. Now they're perfect for a weeknight feed!

SERVES 4

# COCONUT SCHNITZELS WITH RAW APPLE SLAW

4 x 200 g chicken breast fillets

65 g (½ cup) arrowroot or tapioca flour

4 eggs

80 ml (⅓ cup) canned coconut milk

100 g (1 cup) almond meal

100 g (1⅔ cups) shredded coconut

3 teaspoons garlic powder

3 teaspoons smoked paprika

1 teaspoon chilli powder

3 teaspoons dried parsley

sea salt and freshly ground black pepper

coconut oil, for deep-frying

Lemon and Smoked Paprika Aioli (see page 258), to serve

Raw Apple Slaw (see page 114), to serve

lemon wedges, to serve

Working with one piece of chicken at a time, place between two sheets of baking paper. Using a rolling pin or meat mallet, bash the chicken breasts out into flat escalopes about 1–2 cm thick.

Place the flour in a shallow bowl. Whisk the eggs and coconut milk together in a second bowl until well combined. In a third bowl, combine the almond meal, shredded coconut, garlic powder, paprika, chilli powder and parsley. Season with salt and pepper and mix well to combine.

Dip each chicken fillet first into the flour, then into the egg mixture and finally into the almond meal mixture to coat evenly.

Fill a heavy-based saucepan with enough coconut oil for deep-frying and set over medium heat. Heat the oil to 180°C. To test if it is hot enough, simply drop a small piece of bread into the oil – if it sizzles and bubbles you're good to go.

Using tongs, carefully lower the schnitzels into the hot oil in batches. Fry for 6–8 minutes, turning halfway through cooking, until golden brown, then remove from the oil and drain on paper towel. Season generously with salt and pepper and keep warm while you cook the rest.

Divide the schnitzels among plates and serve with some aioli, my raw apple slaw and lemon wedges for squeezing.

While I love any sort of crispy-skinned fish, I probably gravitate towards the oily, pink varieties like salmon and ocean trout out of habit, but mixing it up with a white fish like barramundi is good for both you and your tastebuds. Here, I have paired the barra with a delicious warm tomato and basil salad.

SERVES 4

# CRISPY-SKINNED BARRAMUNDI WITH TOMATO AND BASIL SALAD

4 x 180 g barramundi fillets, skin on
sea salt and freshly ground black pepper
2 tablespoons coconut oil or butter

**Tomato and basil salad**
200 g cherry tomatoes, quartered
3 tablespoons extra-virgin olive oil
zest and juice of 1 lemon
1 large handful of basil leaves, roughly torn

Remove the barra fillets from the fridge and leave to rest on the bench for 5 minutes. Season with salt and pepper.

Heat the coconut oil in a large frying pan over medium heat.

Place the seasoned barra fillets in the pan, skin-side down, and cook for 3–4 minutes, or until the skin is nice and crisp. Use a spatula to gently flip the fillets and cook for another 3–4 minutes, or until cooked through. Remove from the pan, cover loosely with foil and set aside to rest.

To make the tomato and basil salad, add the tomato, olive oil, lemon zest and juice and basil to the pan and stir into the delicious pan juices. Heat gently, stirring, for 1 minute or until warmed through, then serve alongside the delicious fish.

This recipe is a great example of how quick and delicious a meal can be when you've batch-cooked some simple sauces, dressings or, in this case, tzatziki and dukkah! It makes an awesome dish for entertaining, with the cutlets piled up on a platter and with parsley and pomegranate seeds scattered messily over, though it is just as good served simply for a casual weeknight dinner.

SERVES 4

# LUKE'S LAMB CUTLETS WITH TZATZIKI AND DUKKAH

125 g (1 cup) Macadamia Dukkah (see page 264)
12 lamb cutlets
2 tablespoons coconut oil
150 g (½ cup) Minty Paleo Tzatziki (see page 139)

**To serve (optional)**
pomegranate seeds
1 handful of flat-leaf parsley leaves, finely chopped

Place the dukkah in a shallow bowl. Take the lamb cutlets and press them into the dukkah on both sides until they are well coated.

Melt the coconut oil in a large frying pan over medium–high heat. Add the coated cutlets and cook for 3 minutes on each side for medium–rare, for 4 minutes on each side for medium, or until cooked to your liking.

To serve, either divide the lamb cutlets among plates or arrange them on a platter. Top with a generous dollop of tzatziki and scatter over the pomegranate seeds and parsley leaves (if using). Whichever you choose, now's the time to dig in!

## TIP

For those of you who love your Indian flavours, try rubbing these cutlets in my Indian seasoning (see page 265) instead of the dukkah and cook as instructed, then serve with my Coconut and cucumber raita (see page 92) in place of the tzatziki. Yum!

All hail these mighty burgers! Traditionally, Caesar salad is renowned for containing parmesan, but I didn't want non-dairy eaters to miss out so I've finished these burgers off with a lovely 'parmesan' made out of macadamia nuts instead. Whip these up at your next barbecue for a definite crowd pleaser!

SERVES 4

# CHICKEN AND MACADAMIA CAESAR BURGERS

500 g chicken mince
1 bunch of flat-leaf parsley, leaves picked and finely chopped
2 tablespoons macadamia nuts, crushed
1 garlic clove, grated
1 teaspoon garlic powder
1 teaspoon onion powder
2 tablespoons almond meal
1 egg
sea salt and freshly ground black pepper
1–2 tablespoons coconut oil

**To serve**
Less-than-a-minute Mayo (see page 260)
crispy bacon rashers
cos lettuce leaves
macadamia nuts, finely grated

Place the mince, parsley, macadamias, fresh and powdered garlic, onion powder, almond meal and egg in a large bowl. Using your hands, mix everything together really well so that the flavourings are evenly distributed through the mince. Season the mixture well with salt and pepper, then divide into four patties.

Melt the coconut oil in a large frying pan over medium heat, add the patties and fry for about 4–5 minutes on each side, until nicely golden and cooked through. Serve with my mayo, crispy bacon rashers, cos lettuce leaves and finely grated macadamia nut 'parmesan' for a true Caesar experience.

## HEALTH BOOST

Macadamia nuts contain loads of lovely heart-healthy monounsaturated fat, which helps to lower high blood pressure and unhealthy cholesterol levels.

I don't think there are many more traditional or downright delicious flavour combinations than lamb and mint. This burger is a take on my childhood favourite roast lamb with mint sauce. It's such a great combo, and the dairy-free minty tzatziki takes it to the next level!

SERVES 4

# LUSCIOUS LAMB AND MINT BURGERS WITH MINTY PALEO TZATZIKI

500 g lamb mince
1 bunch of mint, leaves picked and finely chopped
1 teaspoon dried rosemary
2 garlic cloves, grated
2 tablespoons almond meal
1 egg
sea salt and freshly ground black pepper
1–2 tablespoons coconut oil

**Minty paleo tzatziki**
4 Lebanese cucumbers, peeled and chopped
1 garlic clove, grated
1 avocado
juice of 1 lemon
2 tablespoons extra-virgin olive oil
3 tablespoons mint leaves, finely chopped
2 teaspoons chopped chives
2 teaspoons dried dill
sea salt and freshly ground black pepper

To make the tzatziki, place the cucumber, garlic, avocado, lemon juice and olive oil in a food processor and pulse until you get a nice thick, creamy texture. Tip the mixture into a bowl, stir in the herbs and season with salt and pepper to taste.

Place the lamb mince, mint, rosemary, garlic, almond meal, egg and a little salt and pepper in a large bowl. Using your hands, mix everything together really well so the flavourings are evenly distributed through the mince. Divide the mixture into four patties.

Melt the coconut oil in a large frying pan over medium heat, add the patties and fry for about 4–5 minutes on each side, until nicely golden and cooked through. Divide among plates and serve with a generous dollop of the minty paleo tzatziki.

## HEALTH BOOST
The aroma of mint activates the salivary glands in our mouth as well as glands which secrete digestive enzymes, thereby facilitating digestion.

Chicken and macadamia Caesar burgers, page 138

Luscious lamb and mint burgers with minty paleo tzatziki, page 139

Pork and fennel burgers, page 143

Beef and chilli burgers with chimichurri, page 142

Some days I just crave a big, juicy beef burger, and this recipe ticks all the right boxes. Generous, flavoursome and fresh, the combination of the patty and chimichurri will make your tastebuds sing! If you're looking to mix things up a bit, this burger can easily be adapted into an Aussie classic. Simply add some freshly grated beetroot and a fried egg, and you've got yourself an outback burger with the lot! This is the perfect Friday night feed in front of the TV.

SERVES 4

# BEEF AND CHILLI BURGERS WITH CHIMICHURRI

600 g beef mince
1 bunch of coriander, leaves picked and finely chopped
1 teaspoon ground cumin
½ teaspoon ground coriander
1 teaspoon sweet paprika
1 teaspoon cayenne pepper
1 long red chilli, finely diced
2 garlic cloves, grated
2 tablespoons almond meal
1 egg
sea salt and freshly ground black pepper
1–2 tablespoons coconut oil
4–8 iceberg lettuce leaves (optional)
1 tomato, sliced

## Chimichurri

2 large handfuls of flat-leaf parsley
2 large handfuls of coriander
3 garlic cloves
1 long red chilli
125 ml (½ cup) extra-virgin olive oil
2 tablespoons apple cider vinegar
juice of 2 lemons
½ teaspoon sea salt

To make the chimichurri, place all the ingredients in a food processor and pulse briefly for 10 seconds or so to form a chunky sauce (be careful not to over-pulse, as you don't want it too smooth). Set aside.

Place the beef mince, coriander, spices, chilli, garlic, almond meal, egg and a little salt and pepper in a large bowl. Using your hands, mix everything together really well so that the flavourings are evenly distributed through the mince. Divide the mixture into four even-sized patties.

Melt the coconut oil in a large frying pan over medium heat, add the patties and fry for about 4–5 minutes on each side, until nicely golden and cooked through. To serve, wrap the patties in the lettuce leaves (if using) and top with some tomato slices and generous dollops of chimichurri.

## TIP

This recipe makes more chimichurri than you need for the burgers – but that's no bad thing! Try stirring it into your scrambled eggs or drizzling it over your roast chicken for an instant boost of zingy, herby flavour. The chimichurri will keep in an airtight container in the fridge for up to 5 days.

Pork and fennel is definitely my favourite type of sausage, and it's this winning combo that gave me the inspiration for this fantastic burger. Fennel has a really interesting flavour that varies depending on whether you are using the fresh fennel bulb, its leafy fronds or the dried seeds. By using the fronds and bulb, this recipe is designed to give you a lovely fennel-y flavour hit. If your bulb doesn't have any fronds, don't worry – just use ground fennel seeds instead.

SERVES 4

# PORK AND FENNEL BURGERS

600 g pork mince
1 bunch of coriander,
    leaves picked and finely
    chopped
1 tablespoon chopped
    fennel fronds or
    1 teaspoon ground
    fennel seeds
½ teaspoon ground
    coriander
1 teaspoon sweet paprika
1 teaspoon cayenne pepper
1 long red chilli, finely diced
2 garlic cloves, grated
2 tablespoons almond meal
1 egg
sea salt and freshly ground
    black pepper
2 tablespoons coconut oil
1 fennel bulb, sliced into
    very thin discs
Raw Apple Slaw (see page
    114), to serve

Place the pork mince, coriander, fennel fronds or seeds, spices, chilli, garlic, almond meal, egg and a little salt and pepper in a large bowl. Using your hands, mix everything together really well so the flavourings are evenly distributed through the mince. Divide the mixture into four patties.

Preheat the oven to 120°C.

Melt the coconut oil in a large, ovenproof frying pan over medium heat, add the patties and fry for about 4–5 minutes on each side, until nicely golden and cooked through. Remove the burgers from the pan, cover with foil and set aside in the oven to keep warm.

Add the fennel discs to the pan and sauté in the pan juices for 10 minutes or until golden brown and softened. Serve alongside the burgers with a few large spoonfuls of my delicious raw apple slaw.

This chilli con carne makes for a perfect post-workout feed or a spicy winter warmer. It celebrates the flavours of Mexico in one easy-to-prepare meal!

SERVES 4

# EASY CHILLI CON CARNE WITH SWEET POTATO CRISPS

2 tablespoons coconut oil
1 onion, finely chopped
1 carrot, grated
½ red capsicum, deseeded and chopped
2 garlic cloves, finely chopped
1 long red chilli, deseeded and finely chopped
600 g beef mince
2 tablespoons Mexican Seasoning (see page 264)
1 x 400 g can diced tomatoes

## Sweet potato crisps
2 sweet potatoes (about 300 g), peeled and sliced into very thin discs using a mandoline
2 tablespoons coconut oil, melted
½ teaspoon paprika
pinch of sea salt

## To serve (optional)
coriander leaves
Paleo Sour Cream (see page 259)
lime wedges

Preheat the oven to 200°C and line two baking trays with baking paper.

For the sweet potato crisps, put the sweet potato slices in a bowl with the coconut oil, paprika and salt and mix well. Arrange the coated slices on the prepared baking trays in a single layer and bake for 10–15 minutes, until crisp and golden brown. Set aside on paper towel to cool.

Melt the coconut oil in a large frying pan over medium heat. Add the onion, carrot, capsicum, garlic and chilli and sauté for about 5 minutes, until softened. Add the beef mince, breaking it up with a wooden spoon. Brown off evenly, then stir in the Mexican marinade and canned tomatoes and simmer for 10 minutes, or until the sauce has thickened and the flavours are well combined.

Spoon the chilli into shallow bowls and serve with the sweet potato crisps. If you feel like fancying things up a bit, scatter over some coriander leaves, dollop over a little paleo sour cream and accompany with lime wedges for squeezing.

Sometimes SIMPLE meals are the BEST meals.

For me, the simplest food is often the most delicious, and that's why I find it hard to look past the classic combo of a well-sourced protein with some clean greens. This recipe is no exception – the addition of the black pepper really brings out the flavour of the meat, and I just love the chimichurri as an accompaniment.

SERVES 4

# PEPPERED STEAKS WITH CHIMICHURRI

4 x 220 g sirloin, scotch
    fillet or rib-eye steaks
1 tablespoon coconut oil
1 teaspoon freshly ground
    black pepper

**To serve**
Chimichurri (see page 142)
green leaves (optional)
lemon wedges

Remove the steaks from the fridge and leave to rest on the bench for 10 minutes to come to room temperature.

Once rested, coat the steaks in the coconut oil and season with the pepper on both sides.

Transfer the steaks to a hot chargrill pan, frying pan or barbecue and cook to your liking – 2 minutes on each side for rare, 2½ minutes for medium and (if you must) 3 minutes on each side for well-done – only flipping them once during cooking.

Remove the steaks from the pan, cover with foil and leave to rest for 5 minutes. Divide the steaks among plates, top with a few generous spoonfuls of chimichurri and serve with your favourite green leaves and lemon wedges for squeezing.

## TIP

Like your pub grub? Well, why not transform this dish into a delicious steak sandwich! Toast up some of my Broccoli breakfast bread (see page 65), add some fresh crunchy greens, sliced tomato and some of my Lemon and smoked paprika aioli (see page 258) and you're good to go!

For years, people used to take the skin off their chicken thinking they were being healthier. Thankfully, we now know that chicken skin contains healthy fats, so you can enjoy its delicious flavours guilt-free. This recipe celebrates that lovely skin in all its glory – just remember, the crispier the better!

SERVES 4

# CRISPY TEXAN CHICKEN

500 g chicken thigh fillets, skin on
1 tablespoon sea salt
2 teaspoons Texan Seasoning (see page 265)
2 teaspoons coconut oil
green leaves, to serve (optional)
Lemon and Smoked Paprika Aioli (see page 258), to serve (optional)

Place the chicken in a bowl. Using your hands, rub the salt and Texan seasoning into the skin so they are seasoned all over.

Melt the coconut oil in a large frying pan over medium heat. Working in manageable batches, add the chicken thighs to the hot pan, skin-side down, and leave to fry, undisturbed, for 6–8 minutes, until the skin is crisp and golden brown and all the fat has rendered. Flip over and fry for a further 3 minutes, or until the chicken is cooked through. Set the cooked chicken aside on paper towel to drain and repeat with the remainder.

To serve, either pile the thighs onto a platter or cut into thick slices and divide among serving plates. Accompany with green leaves and my lemon and smoked paprika aioli, if you like. Dig in!

## TIP

Mixing up the cooking fats here is a great way of exploring different flavours. Try swapping out the coconut oil for butter if you consume dairy, or use a good-quality source of beef tallow, pig lard or duck fat. Each will bring something different to that lovely crispy skin!

# ONE-PAN WONDERS

When I was a kid, we used to celebrate special occasions at the local Chinese restaurant in East Malvern. I used to get so excited about the prawn crackers, lazy Susan and most of all, the special fried rice. Funnily enough, the restaurant still exists and is exactly as it used to be 30 years ago, right down to the neon sign outside – I feel like I should go back for old times' sake! Here's my healthy take on my childhood favourite.

SERVES 4

# SPECIAL FRIED 'RICE'

1 head of cauliflower, roughly chopped

3 tablespoons coconut oil

4 rindless bacon rashers, cut into small cubes

½ onion, finely diced

2.5 cm piece of ginger, grated

1 garlic clove, grated

50 g shiitake or button mushrooms, roughly chopped

2 spring onions, finely sliced, plus extra to serve

3 tablespoons chopped coriander leaves, plus extra to serve

2 tablespoons chopped mint leaves (optional)

1–2 tablespoons coconut aminos (see Tip page 104)

1 teaspoon fish sauce

sea salt and freshly ground black pepper

2 eggs, whisked

1 tablespoon toasted cashew nuts or peanuts, to serve

Place the cauliflower in a food processor and whiz into fine, rice-sized pieces. Set aside.

Melt 2 tablespoons of the coconut oil in a large frying pan or wok over medium–high heat. Add the bacon and stir-fry for 3–4 minutes, until it starts to crisp. Remove from the pan and set aside.

Lower the heat to medium, add the onion, ginger and garlic and stir-fry for 2–3 minutes, until softened, then add the mushroom, spring onion, coriander and mint (if using). Stir-fry for a further 3–4 minutes, then add the cauliflower, coconut aminos and fish sauce to the pan together with the crispy bacon, and season generously with salt and pepper. Sauté for 2–3 minutes until the cauliflower has softened and started to cook through.

Melt the remaining coconut oil in a small frying pan over medium–high heat. Add the egg and swirl around the base of the pan. Cook for about 30 seconds, until the bottom of the egg starts to brown. Flip over and continue cooking for a few more seconds until the omelette is just cooked through. Transfer to a plate, roll up and cut into thin strips.

Divide the fried 'rice' among bowls and serve topped with the toasted nuts, shredded omelette and some extra spring onion and coriander leaves.

## TIP

I love to double up this recipe and pop the extra into lunch boxes for the next day.

## HEALTH BOOST

Cauliflower is part of the cruciferous family of vegetables and is packed full of fantastic nutrients including vitamin C, vitamin B6, manganese and omega-3 fatty acids. To mix things up a little, try making this fried rice with cauliflower's brother-from-another-mother, broccoli!

Have you ever walked through a street market and seen a big traditional paella being made? The aromas are incredible and the flavours just divine. Many of the recipes out there call for all sorts of seafood, but I wanted to strip this Spanish sensation back and make it a little simpler for you to recreate in your own home.

SERVES 4

# PRAWN AND PORK PAELLA

1 head of cauliflower, roughly chopped

2 tablespoons coconut oil or butter

100 g rindless bacon rashers, roughly chopped

200 g chorizo, cut into 2 cm chunks

1 onion, finely chopped

4 garlic cloves, finely chopped

2 tomatoes, roughly diced

1 red capsicum, deseeded and roughly diced

1 long red chilli, deseeded and finely diced

1 tablespoon tomato paste

1 teaspoon smoked paprika, plus extra to serve

500 ml (2 cups) chicken or fish stock (see recipe pages 38–39)

2 pinches of saffron threads

12 raw king prawns, peeled with tails left intact, deveined

sea salt and freshly ground black pepper

1 bunch of flat-leaf parsley, leaves picked and roughly chopped

2 tablespoons extra-virgin olive oil

juice of ½ lemon

Place the cauliflower in a food processor and whiz down to fine, rice-sized pieces. Set aside.

Melt the coconut oil or butter in a large, deep frying pan over medium heat. Add the bacon and chorizo and cook, stirring and tossing the pan as you go, for 5–6 minutes, until the meat has rendered its fat and is nicely caramelised and crisp.

Add the onion, garlic, tomato, capsicum, chilli, tomato paste and paprika to the pan and sauté for 3–4 minutes, or until the vegetables have softened. Pour in the stock, stir in the saffron threads and bring to the boil, then reduce the heat to a simmer, add the prawns and cook for 2–3 minutes, until cooked through. Add the cauliflower and cook, stirring, for a further minute, or until softened. Season with salt and pepper to taste.

Spoon the paella into a serving dish and scatter over the parsley leaves. Drizzle generously with the oil, squeeze over the lemon juice and sprinkle with another pinch or two of smoked paprika. Enjoy!

## TIP

Although I've kept it pretty simple, you can get as creative as you like with your choice of seafood here. Clams, mussels and pipis all work really well, as does calamari. And for those willing to really think outside the paella pan, try it with chicken thighs – you won't look back!

When I travel to Bali, one of the first meals I order is the famous Indonesian *babi guling*, which is usually made with suckling pig. I can't get enough of its aromatic flavours. Taking this great dish as inspiration, I introduce to you… my Seminyak sensation! Now, while this is cooked up in one pan, the spice paste is sneakily whizzed up separately – though, I'm sure you'll forgive me the extra washing up when you taste this!

SERVES 6–8

# SEMINYAK SENSATION

1 kg pork belly, skin on
sea salt
4 parsnips, halved lengthways
2 tablespoons coconut oil, melted
1 handful of coriander leaves, finely chopped, to serve
1 handful of bean sprouts, to serve
1 long red chilli, deseeded and finely chopped, to serve
lime wedges, to serve

### Seminyak spice paste
1 teaspoon sea salt
3 garlic cloves, roughly chopped
3 cm piece of ginger, peeled and finely grated
3 cm piece of fresh turmeric root, peeled and grated
3 bird's eye chillies, deseeded and finely chopped
2 onions, roughly chopped
2 kaffir lime leaves, finely sliced
2 curry leaves, finely sliced
1 tablespoon coriander seeds, crushed
2 tablespoons coconut oil

Prepare the pork belly by patting it dry with paper towel. Season the skin with salt and leave in the fridge for 2–3 hours.

To make the Seminyak spice paste, put all the ingredients in a food processor and whiz together to form a thick paste.

Preheat the oven to 220°C.

Score the pork skin with a knife and then, using your hands, rub the spice paste all over the flesh and skin, being sure to coat it evenly. Place the pork belly skin-side up on a rack set in a roasting tin, and fill the tin with water so that the bottom 2 cm or so of the pork flesh is submerged.

Carefully transfer the tin to the oven and roast for 20 minutes, or until the pork skin is golden and has started to crackle. Reduce the heat to 180°C. Coat the parsnips with the melted coconut oil, season with salt and add to the liquid in the tin. Cook for a further 45–60 minutes, basting the flesh occasionally until the meat is cooked through and the juices run clear when a skewer is inserted into the thickest part.

Remove the pork from the oven and leave to rest for 15 minutes before carving. Serve with the parsnips, coriander, bean sprouts, chilli and a squeeze of fresh lime.

## TIP

This spice paste works really well as a coating for a wide range of proteins – think Balinese-style roast chicken, beef ribs or whole baked fish.

## HEALTH BOOST

Fresh turmeric is full of active compounds called curcuminoids, which contain antioxidant properties that are great for us. Being fat-soluble, they are best absorbed by the body when paired with a healthy fat source, which the coconut oil and the lovely crackly pork skin provide here.

# READ YOUR LABELS

Reading and understanding the labels on packaged food can be a very empowering way of taking your health into your own hands. It can help you determine fact from fiction and make you aware of what you are putting into your body. You'll be surprised by the sneaky marketing tricks some companies use to make you believe something is actually good for you! When it comes to sugar, for example, it's important to understand the different types and be mindful about how much you're having, as excess sugar consumption has been linked to increased risk of type 2 diabetes, fatty liver disease and obesity. Fructose – a sugar molecule that is found naturally but is also present in very high quantities in processed sugars like corn syrup – is the only molecule on the planet that has no corresponding hormone in the brain to tell us when we are full and have had enough, which is why you can devour mountains of sugary foods and have trouble stopping. To make it even tougher, studies have shown foods packed with fructose can lead to an increase in appetite, so not only can we not stop, we keep wanting more of the stuff! So, what can you do to make sure you're not over indulging in the stuff? Read your labels, fill up on good fats and view desserts, even healthy ones, as the occasional treat. And, if you want to know the one way you can avoid reading labels altogether and make healthy easy? Yup, you guessed it, get cooking from scratch at home!

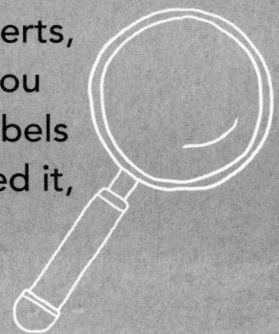

I love breaking up a chook, roasting it with some incredible flavours and scattering it with fresh herbs like this. Not only does it look great, it also doesn't get much tastier in my book! This spice rub is known in the Middle East as 'baharat' and it's a beautiful blend of sweet and smoky spices.

SERVES 4–6

# SMOKY SPICED CHICKEN QUARTERS WITH MOREISH MIDDLE EASTERN SALAD

1 x 1.5 kg chicken, cut into quarters (ask your butcher to do this for you)
2 lemons
4 tablespoons Macadamia Dukkah (see page 264)

**Spice rub**
2 tablespoons coconut oil, melted, plus extra for greasing
3 teaspoons smoked paprika
3 teaspoons ground cumin
2 teaspoons ground coriander
1 teaspoon freshly ground black pepper
½ teaspoon ground cinnamon
½ teaspoon ground nutmeg
pinch of ground cardamom
pinch of ground cloves
1 teaspoon garlic powder

**Middle Eastern salad**
1 bunch of mint, leaves picked
1 bunch of coriander, leaves picked
4 tablespoons extra-virgin olive oil
pinch of sea salt

Get started by preheating the oven to 220°C and lightly greasing a roasting tin with coconut oil.

In a small bowl, mix all the spice rub ingredients together to create a delicious paste. Using your hands, rub this all over the chicken pieces, being sure to get into all the little tight spots. Transfer the chicken to the roasting tin.

Quarter one of the lemons and place underneath the chicken, then squeeze the other lemon all over the top. Roast for 1–1 hour 20 minutes, or until the chicken pieces are lovely and golden and the juices run clear when the thickest part of one of the thighs is pierced with a skewer.

Meanwhile, prepare the Middle Eastern salad. Add the mint and coriander leaves to a bowl, pour over the olive oil and toss well to combine. Season with the salt and toss again.

Once the chicken is cooked, remove it from the oven, cover with foil and leave it to rest for 20 minutes. To serve, pile the salad onto a serving platter, top with the chicken pieces and scatter over the dukkah to finish.

## TIP

Really hungry? Try coating some pumpkin chunks in a little ground cumin and chucking them in the roasting tin 45 minutes before the chicken is ready. Now you're talking!

It doesn't get much BETTER than cooking the chicken on the bone to really bring out the FLAVOURS.

If you're hunting for something to bring some colour and vibrancy to your table, well, look no further than this salmon tarator. My take on this classic dish is slightly different from the traditional version, as I add the herb crust and yoghurt dressing at the end of cooking, which helps gives it a real sense of freshness.

SERVES 4–6

# HERB-CRUSTED SALMON TARATOR WITH TAHINI–YOGHURT DRESSING

1 x 1 kg salmon fillet, skin on and pin-boned
80 ml (⅓ cup) coconut oil, melted
sea salt and freshly ground black pepper
seeds of 1 pomegranate

## Herb crust
1 red onion, finely diced
1 handful of flat-leaf parsley, leaves, finely chopped
1 handful of coriander leaves, finely chopped
1 handful of mint leaves, finely chopped
2 long red chillies, finely chopped
100 g (⅔ cup) macadamia nuts, finely chopped
100 g (1 cup) pecans or walnuts, finely chopped
2 tablespoons sumac
1 tablespoon smoked paprika
150 ml extra-virgin olive oil
sea salt and freshly ground black pepper

## Tahini–yoghurt dressing
200 g coconut yoghurt
90 g (⅓ cup) tahini
juice of 2–3 lemons
2 teaspoons ground cumin
2 garlic cloves, finely diced
½ teaspoon sea salt
½ teaspoon pepper

Get started by preheating the oven to 170°C and lining a large baking tray with baking paper.

Brush the salmon all over with the coconut oil to coat evenly and season generously with salt and pepper. Place the coated fillet skin-side down in the centre of the lined baking tray, then fold over the long sides of baking paper to encase the salmon and twist the ends to seal. Wrap this parcel carefully in foil to retain the heat and place back on the baking tray. Bake for 20–30 minutes, or until the salmon is just cooked through.

While the salmon is baking, make the herb crust and tahini–yoghurt dressing. For the herb crust, combine the ingredients in a bowl and season well with salt and pepper. For the tahini–yoghurt dressing, place all the ingredients in a food processor and pulse until well combined and nice and creamy, loosening it with a tablespoon or two of water, if necessary.

Once the salmon is cooked, remove it from its package and paper and transfer to a large serving platter. Spoon the dressing over the top, then cover with the herb crust. Sprinkle over the pomegranate seeds and enjoy.

## TIP

You can mix this recipe up a little by swapping the salmon for ocean trout if you like. This is a fantastic dish to present at celebratory events – try serving it up with my crunchy Sweet potato skins, Brussels sprout dippers and Sautéed greens (see pages 100, 101 and 108) for a real feast!

Having cooked for myself and my three older brothers for over 30 years, my gorgeous mum is the first to admit that she doesn't love spending too much time in the kitchen these days! When we were growing up though, food, for Mum, was all about keeping her army full and nourished on a tight budget. This chicken cacciatore of hers is a fine example of how cheaper cuts of meat, such as drumsticks, can be cooked low and slow as part of a one-pot hearty braise that seriously delivers on the flavour front.

SERVES 4–6

# MUM'S CHICKEN CACCIATORE

80 ml (⅓ cup) coconut oil or 80 g butter

4 garlic cloves, finely chopped

1 onion, roughly chopped

2 celery stalks, roughly chopped

1.5 kg chicken drumsticks or 1 x 1.5 kg chicken, cut into 8 pieces

500 ml (2 cups) chicken stock (see pages 38–39)

2 x 400 g cans whole peeled tomatoes

1 teaspoon finely chopped thyme leaves

1 teaspoon finely chopped rosemary leaves

1 bay leaf

60 g (½ cup) pitted black olives

1 handful of chopped flat-leaf parsley leaves, plus extra to serve

Preheat the oven to 180°C.

Melt the coconut oil or butter in a flameproof casserole over medium heat. Sauté the garlic, onion and celery for 6–8 minutes, until softened. Add the chicken pieces and cook, turning, for 3–4 minutes, until browned on all sides.

Pour over the chicken stock, add the tomatoes, thyme, rosemary, bay leaf, olives and parsley and bring to the boil. Cover with a lid, transfer to the oven and cook for 45 minutes, turning the chicken pieces occasionally in the liquid, until the chicken is tender and the liquid has reduced to a lovely thick sauce.

To serve, place the casserole on a mat in the centre of the table, top with the extra parsley and let everyone help themselves.

## TIP

Try chucking some sweet potatoes in the oven to bake while this is cooking for a super-easy accompaniment.

I just can't get enough of the flavours of South America. Ingredients like chilli, garlic, coriander, cumin and paprika are all Latin American staples, and the food there is so full of life. Meatballs are up there with fritters for me – I love 'em! You can use any type of mince for this recipe, but I have gone for a combo of beef and pork here because I love the incredible flavour it delivers. The sauce has some kick to it, so feel free to reduce the amount of chilli if you like.

SERVES 4

# SOUTH AMERICAN MEATBALLS WITH SPICY TOMATO SAUCE

250 g beef mince
250 g pork mince
1 egg
1 tablespoon smoked paprika
2 teaspoons ground cumin
1 tablespoon chilli flakes
1 tablespoon chopped flat-leaf parsley leaves
1 tablespoon chopped coriander leaves, plus extra to serve
5 garlic cloves, finely chopped
2 tablespoons coconut oil
1 onion, chopped
1 long red chilli, deseeded and finely chopped
100 ml chicken stock (see recipe pages 38–39) or water
1 teaspoon tomato paste
1 x 400 g can whole peeled tomatoes
1 tablespoon extra-virgin olive oil
Paleo Sour Cream (page 259), to serve
lime wedges, to serve

In a large bowl, combine the beef and pork mince, egg, spices, herbs and three-quarters of the garlic. Mix everything together really well with your hands until it feels as though the meat is binding together with the other ingredients, then roll into balls a little larger than golf balls.

Melt the coconut oil in a large, deep frying pan over medium heat and sauté the onion for 4–5 minutes, until softened and translucent. Stir in the chilli and remaining garlic and sauté for 2 minutes, then add the meatballs and cook for another 2 minutes, or until browned on all sides.

Pour over the chicken stock, add the tomato paste and tomatoes and bring to the boil, then lower the heat to a simmer and cook for 8–10 minutes, or until the sauce has thickened and reduced and the meatballs are cooked through.

To serve, divide the meatballs and spicy tomato sauce among four bowls, scatter over a little extra coriander and drizzle with extra-virgin olive oil. Top with a few dollops of paleo sour cream and serve with lime wedges for squeezing.

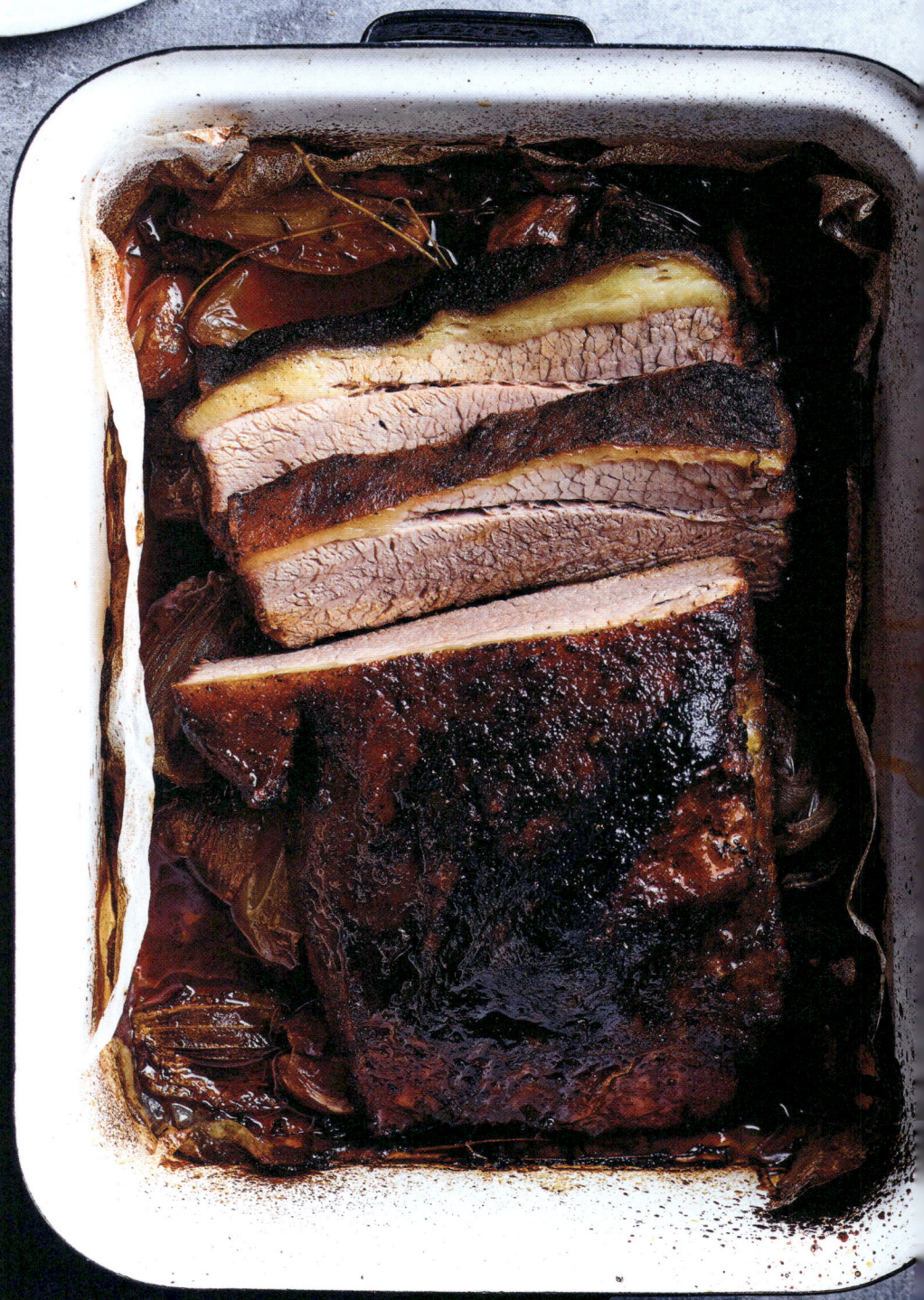

Whenever I go to the States, I love experiencing the barbecue culture and the amazing array of smoked meats I find there. I also love New York's amazing food scene – there are some really interesting things happening across its boroughs, especially in Brooklyn – all of which have come together to inspire this awesome recipe that makes use of delicious brisket. It's super easy and delivers incredible results, making it the perfect way to mix up your Sunday barbecue!

SERVES 8–10

# BROOKLYN BRISKET

1 x 2 kg beef brisket
sea salt and freshly ground
    black pepper
2 tablespoons coconut oil,
    melted
2 onions, quartered
10 garlic cloves, left whole
8–10 thyme sprigs
375 ml (1½ cups) beef stock
    (see recipe pages 38–39)

## Brooklyn spice rub

4 tablespoons smoked
    paprika
2 teaspoons freshly ground
    black pepper
1 teaspoon ground cumin
1 teaspoon cayenne pepper
1 tablespoon sea salt

Get started by preheating the oven or a hooded barbecue to 180°C. Season the brisket well with salt and pepper.

For the spice rub, place all the ingredients in a bowl and mix well to combine.

Add the coconut oil to a deep baking tray, then transfer to the oven until the oil very hot. Carefully remove the tray from the oven, add the brisket to the hot oil and turn to seal on all sides. Transfer the brisket to a board and leave until cool enough to handle, then coat evenly with the spice rub.

Arrange the onion, garlic cloves and thyme sprigs over the bottom of the baking tray in an even layer, top with the brisket and pour over the beef stock. Bake in the oven or under the hood of the barbecue for 20 minutes.

Cover the tray with foil, lower the temperature to 150°C and cook for a further 4 hours, or until the meat is so tender it falls apart when pressed with a fork, checking halfway through cooking and adding up to 125 ml (½ cup) of water if necessary to keep everything nice and moist.

Carve into thick slices and enjoy!

## TIP

If you want to flesh out this meal a little, simply add some root vegetables, such as parsnips, carrots or sweet potato, to the baking tray with the brisket

Being a massive fan of the fiery tastes of South-East Asia, I've given this slow-braised beef dish a bit of a Thai–Balinese twist. Beef cheeks really lend themselves to both slow cooking and the powerful flavours that these cuisines have to offer, so I've used them here to make a dish similar to the traditional Indonesian curry, rendang. I hope you love it as much as I do!

SERVES 4

# BANGKOK BEEF CHEEKS

700–800 g beef cheeks, cut into large chunks
sea salt and freshly ground black pepper
3 tablespoons coconut oil
250 ml (1 cup) canned coconut milk
1 large sweet potato, roughly chopped into chunks
½ butternut pumpkin, roughly chopped into chunks
lime wedges (optional)

**Bangkok spice paste**
1 tablespoon chilli flakes
3 garlic cloves, finely diced
1 onion, roughly chopped
1 tablespoon macadamia nuts
3 cm piece of galangal, peeled and chopped
1 lemongrass stalk, white part only, sliced
2 cm piece of ginger, peeled and chopped
6 kaffir lime leaves, sliced
1 teaspoon coconut sugar
1 teaspoon tamarind juice

**Brauliflower rice**
1 small head of broccoli, roughly chopped
¼ head of cauliflower, chopped
2 tablespoons coconut oil
pinch of sea salt

To make the Bangkok spice paste, simply pulse together all the ingredients in a food processor or pound them together using a mortar and pestle to form a thick, chunky paste.

Season the beef cheeks generously with salt and pepper. Melt 2 tablespoons of the coconut oil in a flameproof casserole dish over medium–high heat, add the seasoned beef cheeks and sauté for 3–4 minutes, or until browned on all sides. Remove the browned beef from the dish with a slotted spoon and set aside.

Add the spice paste to the dish together with the remaining coconut oil and fry it off in all the incredible juices for 4–6 minutes, or until lovely and aromatic. Pour over the coconut milk and bring to the boil, then return the beef to the dish and reduce the heat to very low. Season with salt, cover with a lid and simmer for 4–6 hours, until the meat is very tender, adding the sweet potato and pumpkin 45 minutes before serving.

To make the brauliflower rice, place the chopped broccoli and cauliflower in a food processor and pulse briefly into tiny rice-sized pieces. This usually takes about six to eight pulses – don't over-pulse here as you don't want cauliflower and broccoli dust! Melt the coconut oil in a large frying pan over medium heat, add the cauliflower and broccoli rice and sauté for 4–6 minutes, or until softened.

Remove the lid from the casserole dish and simmer for a final 10–15 minutes, or until the sauce thickens and the meat falls apart when 'cut' with a spoon.

Spoon into serving bowls and enjoy with the brauliflower rice and lime wedges.

One of the most wonderful things my grandmother taught me in the kitchen was how to cook with less popular cuts of meat. As I have mentioned before, offal and other 'non-choice' cuts are loaded with health benefits and lots of great flavour, as well as being easier on the wallet – making them a win-win in my book. These delicious lamb shanks are a sure-fire way to please the whole family. They are great on their own or with some simple steamed greens.

SERVES 4

# NAN'S SLOW-COOKED LAMB SHANKS

2 tablespoons coconut oil
4 x 250 g lamb shanks
sea salt
1 onion, roughly chopped
4 garlic cloves, roughly chopped
1 long red chilli, deseeded and roughly chopped
2 carrots, roughly chopped
1 large sweet potato, roughly chopped
500 ml (2 cups) tomato passata
2 tablespoons tomato paste
750 ml (3 cups) beef stock (see pages 38–39)
1 fresh or dried bay leaf
1 tablespoon fresh or dried oregano leaves
4 rosemary sprigs
freshly ground black pepper
chopped flat-leaf parsley leaves, to serve (optional)
steamed greens, to serve

Melt the coconut oil in a large, heavy-based saucepan or flameproof casserole dish over high heat.

Season the lamb shanks generously with salt, add them to the pan and sauté for 3–4 minutes, or until sealed and browned on all sides. Remove from the pan with a slotted spoon and set aside.

Add the onion, garlic and chilli to the pan and sauté in all the lovely lamb juices for 3 minutes, or until soft and caramelised. Add the carrot and sweet potato and cook for a further 2 minutes. Return the lamb shanks to the pan and add the tomato passata, tomato paste and beef stock. Stir through the bay leaf, oregano and rosemary and season with salt and pepper. Bring to the boil, then reduce the heat to very low, cover with a lid and simmer very gently for 6–8 hours, or until the meat falls apart when pressed with a fork.

Divide among plates, scatter over a little parsley (if using) and serve with your choice of steamed greens.

## TIP

This is a great dish to cook up in bulk and keep in the freezer for those nights when you find yourself without much time but craving something really nourishing and warming.

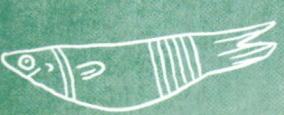

# SURF

I love this dish as it can be on the table in less than 15 minutes, and because it celebrates a super-tasty, oily fish. Mackerel is a fantastic fish to incorporate into your diet. It's packed full of healthy omega-3 fatty acids – which are great for our overall wellbeing – plus it's a sustainable choice.

SERVES 4

# LEMONY GRILLED MACKEREL FILLETS WITH GREMOLATA

8 x mackerel fillets, skin on
sea salt and freshly ground
    black pepper
2 tablespoons coconut oil,
    melted
zest and juice of 1 lemon
65 g (⅓ cup) Great
    Gremolata (see page 260)
fresh rocket leaves, to serve

Heat a chargrill pan or barbecue to medium–high.

Season the mackerel fillets generously with salt and pepper and rub them on both sides with the coconut oil.

Place the mackerel fillets skin-side down on the chargrill pan or barbecue grill, cover with foil and cook for 2–3 minutes, until the skin is golden brown. Using a spatula, give them a flip and cook for a further 4 minutes, or until the fish is completely opaque throughout.

Divide the grilled fish fillets among plates and scatter over the lemon zest. Squeeze over the lemon juice, spoon over the gremolata and serve with rocket on the side.

## HEALTH BOOST

As well as being stuffed full of omega-3 fatty acids, oily fish like mackerel are a great source of protein and essential nutrients like vitamin D. Chowing down on these fish has also been linked to a number of health benefits, including a lower risk of heart disease, improved mental ability and protection from cancer, dementia and arthritis. So what are you waiting for? It's time to get eating!

Salmon is a real go-to ingredient for me. I'm always looking for new ways to enjoy it, as it's pretty easy to get stuck in a bit of a rut when cooking it. Luckily, that's where this Jamaican glaze comes in – it brings so much flavour to your plate! If you're not massively keen on spice, don't worry too much, as the freshness of the pineapple and avocado salsa helps to cut through the chilli heat.

SERVES 4

# JAMAICAN JERK SALMON WITH PINEAPPLE AND AVOCADO SALSA

4 x 180 g salmon fillets, skin on
1 x quantity Pineapple and Avocado Salsa (see page 262)
2 tablespoons toasted crushed cashew nuts

### Jamaican jerk glaze

2 spring onions, finely chopped
2 garlic cloves, finely chopped
1 long red chilli, finely diced
3 tablespoons coconut sugar
2 tablespoons coconut aminos (see Tip page 104)
2 tablespoons coconut oil, melted
zest and juice of 2 limes
1 teaspoon dried thyme
pinch of ground allspice
pinch of ground cinnamon
sea salt and freshly ground black pepper

Preheat the oven to 200°C and line a baking tray with baking paper.

To make the jerk glaze, place all the ingredients in a food processor or blender and whiz together until well combined. Season to taste with salt and pepper, pour the mixture into a small bowl and set aside.

Arrange the salmon fillets skin-side down on the prepared baking tray and coat well with the jerk glaze. Transfer to a rack in the centre of the oven and bake for 6–8 minutes, or until the fish is tender and just cooked through.

Divide the salmon fillets and the pineapple and avocado salsa among serving plates, scatter over the crushed toasted cashews and serve.

## TIP

This jerk glaze doesn't just taste delicious with salmon, it's great with meat, too. Double up the recipe and store the extra in the fridge (it will keep in a suitable container for up to 7 days) for spreading over chicken wings or pork ribs before cooking. Yum!

This dish is on HIGH
ROTATION at my place, and
you'll soon see why!

I have very fond memories of enjoying this salad on the beaches in the south of France when I was a young backpacker – though it took me until just a few years ago to actually work out how to pronounce the name! Back then it was the one meal I could afford, which wasn't a problem as there's so much to love in this super-fresh plate of awesomeness. I think this recipe is a great example of the incredible flavours you can enjoy when eating clean.

SERVES 4

# TANTALISING TUNA NIÇOISE WITH VIBRANT VINAIGRETTE

4 eggs
2 large fennel bulbs, very finely sliced
80 ml (⅓ cup) coconut oil, melted
sea salt and freshly ground black pepper
1 bunch of asparagus, trimmed and cut into 5 cm lengths
200 g cherry tomatoes, halved
100 g pitted black olives
8 white anchovy fillets
2 teaspoons capers, rinsed and roughly chopped
½ red onion, finely sliced
400 g good-quality canned tuna in brine or olive oil, drained and broken into chunks

## Vibrant vinaigrette
125 ml (½ cup) extra-virgin olive oil
1 garlic clove, crushed
1 teaspoon dijon mustard
2 tablespoons apple cider vinegar
zest and juice of 1 lemon
2 tablespoons chopped flat-leaf parsley leaves
2 tablespoons chopped tarragon leaves

Preheat the oven to 180°C. Line a baking tray with baking paper.

Place the eggs in a small saucepan and cover with cold water. Cover with a lid and bring to the boil, then reduce the heat to medium and simmer gently for 3 minutes. Remove the eggs from the pan and leave to cool, then peel and cut in half.

Arrange the fennel slices on the prepared baking tray in a single layer, drizzle over the coconut oil and season well with salt and pepper. Roast in the oven for 10–15 minutes, stirring and tossing occasionally, until lightly golden and cooked through. Set aside to cool.

Meanwhile, set a steamer over a small saucepan filled with a little water and bring to the boil. Add the asparagus, cover with a lid and steam for 3–5 minutes, until tender. Set aside to cool.

To make the vinaigrette, combine all the ingredients in a bowl and whisk well.

To assemble the salad, combine the roasted fennel, steamed asparagus, tomato, olives, anchovies, capers and onion in a large bowl. Season with salt and pepper, add just enough dressing to moisten the ingredients and toss gently to coat.

Pile the salad onto a serving platter or individual plates and top with the tuna and soft-boiled eggs. Drizzle over a little extra vinaigrette, if you like, then tuck in!

## HEALTH BOOST

I like to use apple cider vinegar in my vinaigrettes, as it helps to balance our stomach acid's pH level, encourages the growth of healthy bacteria and combats the growth of harmful gut flora – the micro-organisms that live in your mouth and intestines.

I love a good fishcake, and they're super quick and easy to make at home. I've celebrated Thai flavours in this recipe, but you could whip them up with whatever herb and spice flavour combination you prefer. I like to make these up in big batches and freeze the extras to enjoy down the track.

SERVES 4

# SPICY FISHCAKES IN CRUNCHY LETTUCE CUPS

500 g whiting or snapper fillets, skin removed, pin-boned and diced

2 garlic cloves, finely chopped

1 tablespoon fish sauce

1 long red chilli, roughly chopped

1 red onion, roughly chopped

2 tablespoons coconut cream

sea salt and freshly ground black pepper

80 ml (⅓ cup) coconut oil, melted

2 tablespoons sesame seeds

**To serve**

4 iceberg lettuce leaves

100 g bean sprouts

1 carrot, cut into matchsticks

1 Lebanese cucumber, deseeded and cut into matchsticks

1 handful of coriander leaves, chopped

2 tablespoons roughly chopped toasted cashew nuts

juice of 1 lime

Add the fish pieces to a food processor and pulse briefly to combine. Add the garlic, fish sauce, chilli, red onion and coconut cream and continue to pulse until you end up with a nice, thick paste. Season well with salt and pepper.

Brush your hands with a teaspoon or so of the coconut oil (this will stop everything from sticking to them), then divide the fish mixture into four equal-sized patties.

Place the sesame seeds in a shallow bowl, then press the fishcakes into the seeds until lightly coated on all sides.

Heat the remaining coconut oil in a chargrill pan, frying pan or on a barbecue plate over medium heat. Cook the patties for 6–8 minutes, turning halfway through cooking, until golden brown and cooked through.

To serve, arrange the lettuce leaves on a serving platter. Place a fishcake in the centre of each lettuce cup and top with some bean sprouts, carrot, cucumber, coriander, toasted cashew nuts and a squeeze of lime juice.

## TIP

I love the way that herbs and spices can take healthy cooking to the next level – they're affordable, delicious and can be added to almost any dish. Try mixing them up here to come up with your own fishcake recipes – I like making Middle Eastern fishcakes by using sumac, cumin and ground coriander, while ground turmeric, garam masala and dried chilli make a fantastic Indian-spiced alternative.

This is a fantastic, quick and easy recipe that the whole family will love. Get the kids to help you make the batter – cooking's always more fun when everyone gets involved!

# PHENOMENAL FISH BITES WITH LEMON AND SMOKED PAPRIKA AIOLI

400 g whiting or snapper fillets, skin removed and pin-boned
60 g (½ cup) arrowroot or tapioca flour
2 eggs, whisked
100 g (1 cup) almond meal
½ teaspoon sea salt
½ teaspoon sweet paprika
80 ml (⅓ cup) coconut oil
lemon wedges, to serve
Lemon and Smoked Paprika Aioli (see page 258), to serve

Cut the fish fillets into pieces roughly 1.5 cm wide and 10 cm long.

Place the flour in one bowl, the egg in another and the almond meal, salt and paprika in a third bowl.

Dip the fish pieces first in the flour, then the egg and finally into the almond meal mixture to coat well on all sides.

Heat the coconut oil in a large frying pan over medium heat. Add the fish to the pan, spacing them apart, and cook for 3–4 minutes on each side, until golden brown (you may need to do this in batches so as not to overcrowd the pan).

Remove the fish bites from the pan and drain oil on paper towel. Serve with lemon wedges and a bowl of lemon and smoked paprika aioli for dipping.

# FAD DIETS

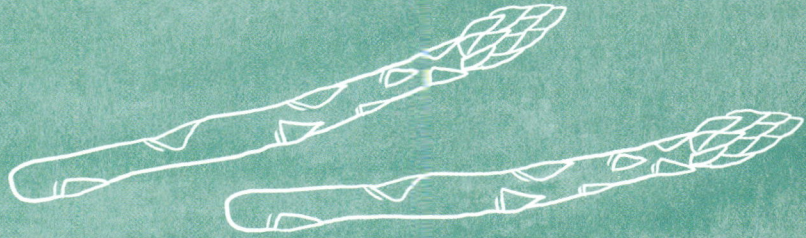

To be truly healthy, we need to make small, sustainable and enjoyable incremental changes that lead to building life-long healthy habits. That's why I am not a fan of quick fixes, short cuts or fad diets – anything short-term, drastic or restrictive just won't work, and you won't enjoy it either. Turning your health around *should* be fun guys, and there's absolutely no reason why you can't still enjoy some of your favourite foods in moderation, or with a healthier twist along the way. As with anything in life, we are way more likely to stick to something if we are having fun doing it. I want this health journey to be something you really look forward to each and every day and not something that makes you nervous or stressed. It is about celebrating that healthy relationship with food I always talk about, listening to your body and doing what works for you and your lifestyle. If you love the process, make it fun and are always able to have a laugh at yourself, then you're well on your way to being the best version of yourself through real food. Steer clear of the overnight before and afters, magic pills or drastic decisions, and remember that healthy made easy starts when it's realistic. So keep it real, legends.

In my previous book, *Eat Clean*, I shared some of my favourite curries, but looking back I realise they all starred beef or poultry! That's why I wanted to share this quick fish curry – another of my all-time faves – with you. The coconut naan bread here is a fantastic flavoursome accompaniment, perfect for scooping up any leftover sauce you may have in your bowl.

SERVES 4

# BUTTER BARRAMUNDI WITH COCONUT NAAN BREAD

2 tablespoons coconut oil

1 onion, roughly chopped

4 garlic cloves, finely chopped

1 tomato, roughly chopped

1 red capsicum, deseeded and roughly chopped

1 long red chilli, chopped

1 teaspoon garam masala

1 teaspoon ground cumin

1 teaspoon ground coriander

1 teaspoon ground turmeric

1 teaspoon hot chilli powder

2 x 270 ml cans coconut cream

600 g barramundi fillet, skin removed and cut into large chunks

Brauliflower Rice (see page 170), to serve (optional)

## Coconut naan bread

100 g (1 cup) almond meal

125 g (1 cup) arrowroot or tapioca flour

125 ml (½ cup) canned coconut milk

125 ml (½ cup) filtered water

pinch of sea salt

coconut oil, for frying

For the coconut naan bread, combine all the ingredients except the oil in a bowl and mix well to form a smooth batter.

Melt 1–2 tablespoons of the coconut oil in a small non-stick frying pan over medium heat. Add a quarter of the batter and swirl the pan to ensure it evenly coats the base. Cook for 2–3 minutes, then carefully flip with a spatula and cook for a further 2 minutes, or until golden and cooked through. Repeat with the remaining batter, greasing the pan with coconut oil in between naans to make sure they don't stick to the pan. Set aside wrapped in a clean tea towel to keep warm.

Melt the coconut oil in large, deep frying pan over medium–high heat. Add the onion and garlic and sauté for 2–3 minutes, until softened and lightly golden, then add the tomato, capsicum and chilli and cook, stirring, until lightly browned on all sides.

Stir in the spices and cook for another 2–3 minutes. Pour over the coconut cream, bring to a simmer and cook over medium heat for 4 minutes, or until the sauce has thickened and reduced slightly, then add the barramundi and cook for 5–7 minutes, or until the fish is cooked through and all the flavours have melded together.

Divide the brauliflower rice (if using) among bowls, spoon over the curry and serve with the coconut naan.

## TIP

Try making up a big batch of the naan bread – the leftovers will keep in an airtight container in the fridge for up to 1 week or in the freezer for up to 3 months.

Cool, refreshing and full of flavour, this is such a fantastic recipe for the summer months. It reminds me of balmy nights in Asia spent sitting and watching the sunset. It's nice and versatile too – try swapping out the ocean trout for salmon, barramundi, or even poached chicken!

SERVES 4

# CHILLED COCONUT OCEAN TROUT WITH CHILLI AND LIME DIPPING SAUCE

1 x 400 ml can coconut cream

zest and juice of 2 limes

6 kaffir lime leaves (optional)

generous pinch of sea salt

4 x 180 g ocean trout fillets, skin removed and pin-boned

1 green papaya (about 800 g), peeled, deseeded and shredded

1 bunch of coriander, leaves picked

juice of 1 lime

2 tablespoons roughly chopped toasted cashew nuts

**Chilli and lime dipping sauce**

juice of 1½ limes

1 teaspoon fish sauce

2 teaspoons coconut aminos (see Tip page 104)

1 teaspoon coconut nectar

1 long green chilli, deseeded and finely chopped

generous pinch of sea salt

Add the coconut cream, lime zest and juice, lime leaves (if using) and salt to a large non-stick frying pan over very low heat and stir to combine. Bring to a gentle simmer, stirring occasionally and making sure the liquid doesn't boil or catch on the bottom of the pan, then lower in the ocean trout fillets and poach gently for 6–8 minutes, turning halfway, until cooked through. Remove the pan from the heat and leave to cool slightly, then transfer the trout pieces and poaching liquid to a suitable airtight container and leave to chill in the fridge.

To make the chilli and lime dipping sauce, place all the ingredients in a bowl and whisk to combine.

Once chilled, remove the fish fillets from the poaching liquid and arrange on a serving platter or individual serving plates. Pile the papaya next to the fish and top with the coriander, a drizzle of the poaching liquid and the lime juice. Scatter over the toasted cashews and serve with the dipping sauce on the side.

PARSLEY

# TURF

Yep, you heard me right ladies and gentlemen! Chips made out of bacon. Need I say more?

SERVES 4

# CRISPY BACON CHIPS WITH GUACAMOLE

500 g rindless streaky
  bacon rashers
1 x quantity Gorgeous
  Guacamole (see
  page 258)

Preheat the oven to 200°C and line one large baking tray or two small baking trays with baking paper.

Place the bacon in a single layer on the prepared tray/s, making sure the strips are not touching. Bake, turning the tray around halfway through for even cooking, for about 15 minutes, until the bacon is golden and crisp.

Allow the bacon to cool completely then cut into rough shards to enjoy with the guacamole or your other favourite dips. Best enjoyed fresh.

## HEALTH BOOST

The healthy fats found in avocado and bacon are great for helping reduce inflammation and joint pain and for promoting a healthy hormone balance, especially if the bacon you use is sourced from free-range pigs and is nitrate free.

I have been a fan of chicken satay skewers ever since I was a kid and my parents first took me to a Thai restaurant. Here, the richness of the cashew satay really cuts through the heat of the chilli, with the whole thing set off by a refreshing squeeze of fresh lime. Give it a try – your tastebuds will be sure to thank you.

SERVES 4

# SEXY SATAY CHICKEN SKEWERS

800 g chicken thigh fillets, cut into 2.5 cm cubes
sea salt and freshly ground black pepper
coriander leaves, to serve
lime halves, to serve

**Marinade**

2 tablespoons coconut oil, melted
zest and juice of 2 limes
2 tablespoons coconut aminos (see Tip page 104)
1 tablespoon fish sauce
2 garlic cloves, finely diced
2 cm piece of ginger, peeled and finely grated
1 tablespoon ground turmeric
1 teaspoon maple syrup (optional)

**Sexy satay sauce**

150 g cashew nuts
150 g almond butter
2 tablespoons coconut aminos
3 cm piece of ginger, peeled and finely grated
1 long red chilli, deseeded and finely chopped
1 tablespoon extra-virgin olive oil or avocado oil
1 tablespoon maple syrup
3 tablespoons filtered water, plus extra if needed
pinch of sea salt

Place eight bamboo skewers in a shallow dish, cover with cold water and leave to soak for at least 30 minutes.

To make the marinade, place all the ingredients in a large bowl and whisk together well. Add the chicken pieces and toss until well coated, then transfer to the fridge and leave to marinate for at least 30 minutes (or up to 2 hours).

For the satay sauce, combine all the ingredients in a food processor and blend until smooth. If the sauce is a little too thick, simply add a little more water. Set aside.

Preheat a barbecue, chargrill pan or frying pan over medium heat.

Thread the marinated chicken cubes onto the prepared skewers and season well with salt and pepper. Grill the skewers, basting with the marinade as you go, for about 3 minutes on each side, until cooked through and nicely charred on the outside.

Transfer the skewers to a serving platter, season with salt and pepper and scatter over the coriander leaves. Serve with the satay dipping sauce and lime halves.

Some nights all I feel like for dinner is a steak and salad, and I'm sure I'm not alone. I like mine nice and simple – after all, why trick something up that doesn't need it? Simple flavours speak for themselves. For me, a dinner that tastes great and is good for you is what cooking is all about!

SERVES 2

# SIMPLE SIRLOIN WITH BACON AND MUSHIES

2 x 220 g sirloin steaks
2 tablespoons coconut oil or butter, melted
sea salt and freshly ground black pepper
100 g streaky bacon rashers, cut into small squares
200 g mushrooms, quartered or halved
2 garlic cloves, finely chopped
2 thyme sprigs, leaves picked
2 handfuls of rocket or baby kale leaves
2 tablespoons chopped flat-leaf parsley leaves
3 tablespoons extra-virgin olive oil or avocado oil
2 lemons, cut into wedges
1 tablespoon grated fresh horseradish or wholegrain mustard

Remove the steaks from the fridge and leave on the bench for 10 minutes to come to room temperature.

Once rested, coat the steaks in 1 teaspoon of the coconut oil and season with a generous pinch of salt and some pepper.

Preheat a barbecue, chargrill pan or frying pan over high heat. Add the steaks and cook to your liking – 2 minutes on each side for rare, 2½ minutes for medium and (if you must) 3 minutes on each side for well-done – only flipping them once during cooking. Remove the steaks from the pan, cover with foil and leave to rest for at least 5 minutes, or until you're ready to plate up.

Meanwhile, add the remaining coconut oil to the pan juices together with the bacon, mushroom, garlic and thyme and sauté for 4 minutes, or until the bacon is cooked and the mushroom is lovely and soft. Season generously with pepper and set aside.

In a bowl, toss the rocket or kale and parsley with the olive oil and a squeeze of lemon juice from one of the wedges. Season with salt and pepper.

Divide the steaks between plates, sprinkle over the horseradish or spread with the mustard and serve with the rocket and parsley salad, sautéed bacon and mushrooms, and lemon wedges on the side.

## TIP

If you've rested the steaks after cooking for longer than 5 minutes, you might want to place them back on the barbecue, chargrill or pan for 15 seconds on each side to warm up slightly just before serving.

This recipe is a shining example of what a few cleverly used ingredients and a good cooking technique can do to a plain piece of meat. The thick, succulent pork chops are seared, then roasted, then slathered with sweet glaze and returned to the oven until perfectly caramelised. Delicious!

SERVES 4

# PERFECT PORK CHOPS WITH GLISTENING GLAZE

4 x 220 g bone-in pork chops
sea salt and freshly ground black pepper
2 tablespoons coconut oil or butter
Raw Apple Slaw (see page 114), to serve

### Glistening glaze
2 tablespoons coconut aminos (see Tip page 104)
2 tablespoons maple syrup, honey or coconut nectar
2 garlic cloves, finely chopped
1 teaspoon dried rosemary
1 teaspoon dried oregano
pinch of chilli flakes

Preheat the oven to 200°C.

Give the pork chops a generous seasoning with salt and pepper and set aside on the bench to warm to room temperature.

For the glaze, combine all the ingredients in a small saucepan and bring to the boil over medium heat. Lower the heat to a simmer and cook for about 5 minutes, until reduced to a thick, sticky glaze. Set aside.

Melt the coconut oil in a large, cast-iron frying pan over medium heat until smoking, add the pork chops and sear for 2 minutes on each side, or until lovely and golden. Transfer the pan to the middle of the oven and roast for 5 minutes, then brush the pork chops on both sides with the prepared glaze and roast for a further 4 minutes, or until caramelised and gorgeous! Serve alongside my raw apple slaw.

When it comes to cooking with meat I love chicken wings, as they are super affordable and super tasty. This recipe celebrates them and is such a great way to get the health benefits of turmeric into your diet. It's also excellent if you're cooking for a big group – just multiply the quantities as needed and get piling those wings up nice and high!

SERVES 4

# SUPER-TASTY TURMERIC CHICKEN WINGS

1 kg chicken wings
80 ml (⅓ cup) coconut oil, melted

**Turmeric marinade**

3 tablespoons ground turmeric
2 tablespoons ground coriander
2 tablespoons ground cumin
1 teaspoon chilli powder, or to taste
1 teaspoon sea salt
3 tablespoons coconut aminos (see Tip page 104)
3 garlic cloves, finely chopped
3 cm piece of ginger, peeled and finely grated

**To serve**

coriander leaves (optional)
lime wedges
coconut and cucumber raita (see page 192) (optional)

To make the marinade, add the spices and salt to a bowl and mix well. In a separate large bowl, mix together the coconut aminos, garlic and ginger.

Add the chicken wings to the coconut aminos mixture then tip the spice mixture over the top. Massage the marinade into the chicken wings with your hands, making sure they are well coated, then cover the bowl with plastic wrap, transfer to the fridge and leave to marinate for 2–12 hours. (The longer you leave them the more the flavours will develop.)

When you're ready to cook, preheat the oven to 180°C and line a deep baking dish or tin with baking paper.

Place the chicken wings in the prepared baking dish in a single layer, brush with the melted coconut oil and pour over 80 ml of water. Roast in the oven for 45 minutes, turning halfway through cooking, until cooked through and nice and golden brown all over.

Pile the wings onto a large share platter, scatter over some fresh coriander (if using) and serve with lime wedges and my coconut and cucumber raita, if you like.

With its golden, crispy exterior and flavoursome, salty filling the Chiko Roll has been described as an Australian cultural icon. At the peak of their popularity in the 1960s and '70s over 40 million of them were sold annually! These paleo rolls are your gluten-free, dairy-free answer to this famous Aussie takeaway-night staple.

MAKES 4

# PALEO CHIKO ROLLS

2 teaspoons coconut oil
  or butter
1 onion, finely sliced
¼ green cabbage, outer
  leaves removed, thinly
  shredded
1 celery stalk, finely sliced
1 carrot, grated
250 g lamb mince
1 tablespoon arrowroot
  or tapioca flour
1 egg, lightly whisked
Garlicky No-tomato Pasta
  Sauce, to serve (see
  page 254)

**Pastry**
200 g (2 cups) almond meal
2 eggs
3 tablespoons coconut oil,
  melted
pinch of baking powder

To make the pastry, combine the almond meal, eggs, coconut oil and baking powder in a bowl and mix well to form a nice, wet dough. Roll into a ball, wrap in plastic wrap and transfer to the fridge to chill for 30 minutes.

Meanwhile, melt the coconut oil or butter in a frying pan over medium heat. Add the onion, cabbage, celery and carrot and cook for 6–8 minutes, until soft. Add the lamb and brown on all sides, then stir in the flour and mix everything together to get rid of any lumps.

Preheat the oven to 180°C and line a baking tray with baking paper.

Remove the pastry from the fridge and break it into four equal-sized balls. Working with one dough ball at a time, roll it out between two sheets of baking paper into a rectangle about 5 mm thick. Remove the top sheet of baking paper and, using a sharp knife, trim the pastry into a neat rectangle, reserving the excess pastry as you go. Repeat with the remaining dough balls.

Spread the filling evenly among the prepared pastry sheets. Starting at one of the longer sides, carefully roll the pastry up, then, using a pastry brush, seal the edges with the whisked egg.

Use the leftover pastry scraps to seal the ends of each piece, then carefully transfer them to the prepared baking tray, seam-side down, and bake in the oven for 30–40 minutes, until beautiful and golden brown. Leave to cool slightly before serving with my garlicky no-tomato sauce.

I first made a version of this dish when I was on *My Kitchen Rules,* and I remember the episode clearly, as I had my first TV cry. We had just managed to plate everything up with no time left on the clock, only to find out that the lamb was possibly raw in the middle. It was an agonising wait, watching the judges cut into the meat to see that it was only just cooked … but passable! I assure you this version is far more than passable – in fact, it's perfect for a family celebration.

SERVES 4–6

# HERB-CRUSTED LAMB RACK ON CAULIFLOWER PUREE

2 x 1 kg french-trimmed lamb racks (about 3–4 cutlets per person)
sea salt and freshly ground black pepper
2 large handfuls of mint leaves
2 large handfuls of flat-leaf parsley leaves
100 g (1 cup) pecans or walnuts
2 garlic cloves
1 tablespoon dijon mustard
3 tablespoons extra-virgin olive oil or avocado oil
2 tablespoons coconut oil or butter
1 handful of micro herbs, for garnish (optional)

**Cauliflower puree**
1 head of cauliflower, stalk removed and florets chopped
80 ml (⅓ cup) coconut oil or 80 g butter or ghee
3 garlic cloves, grated
pinch of sea salt

Get started by preheating the oven to 180°C and lining a baking tray with baking paper.

Cut the lamb racks into individual serving portions. Season well with salt and pepper and set aside on the bench to come to room temperature.

Place the herbs, pecans or walnuts, garlic, mustard, olive oil and 1 teaspoon of salt in a food processor and whiz together to form a thick, chunky paste.

Melt the coconut oil or butter in a large frying pan over high heat. Add the lamb portions and brown off briefly on all sides, then transfer to a plate and leave to cool. Once cool, spread the herb paste over the meaty top of the rack portions, pressing it down with your fingers to compact it nicely.

Arrange the lamb portions on the prepared baking tray and roast for 12–15 minutes, until the lamb is cooked through but still nicely pink (cut into one of the lamb portions with a sharp knife to check). Remove the lamb from the oven and leave to rest, uncovered, for 5 minutes.

Meanwhile, to make the cauliflower puree, steam or boil the cauliflower florets until soft, then transfer to a food processor with the coconut oil, butter or ghee, garlic and salt. Pulse until well combined and smooth.

To serve, spoon the cauliflower puree onto the centre of your serving plates and arrange the lamb portions on top. Drizzle over the lovely lamb cooking juices from the tray and scatter over the micro herbs to finish, if you like. Enjoy!

If you are able to get your hands on some top-quality grass-fed beef then this is the ultimate way to eat it. Not only does it taste delicious but – being served raw – it's very good for you too, as no nutrients are lost in the cooking process. I like my tartare served with some crisp celeriac chips on the side to use as little scoops for each tasty mouthful.

SERVES 4

# BRILLIANT BEEF TARTARE WITH CELERIAC CRISPS

4 anchovy fillets in olive oil, drained and finely chopped

1 tablespoon capers, rinsed

2 tablespoons dijon mustard

2 egg yolks

600 g beef tenderloin, cut into small dice, covered, and refrigerated until ready to use

¼ red onion, finely chopped

2 tablespoons finely chopped flat-leaf parsley leaves

1 tablespoon extra-virgin olive oil

4 dashes of tabasco sauce

4 dashes of worcestershire sauce

1 teaspoon chilli flakes (optional)

sea salt and freshly ground black pepper

**Celeriac crisps**

2 celeriac (about 450 g), peeled and sliced into very thin discs

80 ml (⅓ cup) coconut oil, melted

sea salt

1 tablespoon sweet paprika

Preheat the oven to 200°C and line two baking trays with baking paper.

For the celeriac crisps, put the celeriac slices in a bowl with the coconut oil and 1 teaspoon of salt and mix together well. Arrange the coated slices on the prepared baking trays in a single layer and bake for 10–15 minutes, until crispy and golden brown. Once they're cooked, sprinkle with the paprika and a little extra salt, and set aside on paper towel to cool.

Place the anchovies, capers and mustard in a large bowl and mix well with a fork. Add the egg yolks and mix again to combine, then fold in the remaining ingredients. Mix everything together again to ensure it is thoroughly combined and season generously with salt and pepper.

To serve, spoon the tartare onto a serving platter and serve with the celeriac crisps.

## TIP

Because you will be serving the meat raw, be sure to buy it from a reputable source, and tell your butcher that you will be preparing it as tartare so he or she gives you the best cut. Also, as you'll be eating the yolk raw, you should only use the freshest, highest-quality eggs here, too.

# SWEETS

An easy and delicious raw chocolate is such a great thing to have in your clean-treat repertoire. It's a really versatile little staple that can be turned into a multitude of delicious bites!

MAKES 350 G (2 CUPS)

# RAD RAW CHOCOLATE

220 g (1 cup) cacao butter
120 g (1 cup) cacao powder
3 tablespoons maple syrup
1 vanilla pod, split and
    seeds scraped

Stir all the ingredients together in a saucepan over low heat until lovely and runny.

Use it in its melted state to top or dip desserts, or pour over a baking tray lined with baking paper and set in the freezer for about 30 minutes for a basic chocolate slab.

Store in a suitable airtight container in the fridge for up to 1 month or in the freezer for up to 3 months.

I love roasting strawberries as it brings out the most incredible flavour! If you haven't got much of a sweet tooth or are avoiding added sugars, simply omit the maple syrup from the recipe and you will still be left with the most delicious of dessert accompaniments.

MAKES 250 G (1 CUP)

# ROASTED STRAWBERRIES

400 g strawberries, hulled
1 tablespoon maple syrup
    (optional)
1 vanilla pod, split and
    seeds scraped

Preheat the oven to 180°C and line a baking tray with baking paper.

Place the strawberries, maple syrup (if using) and vanilla seeds in a bowl and stir gently to coat well. Arrange the strawberries on the prepared baking tray in an even layer and roast for 15–20 minutes, or until soft and caramelised. Allow to cool, then store in an airtight container in the fridge for up to 7 days.

This versatile whipped coconut cream is super delicious – try it spooned on top of your breakfast, dolloped into a hot drink or served alongside your favourite dessert.

MAKES ABOUT 250 ML (1 CUP)

# WHIPPED VANILLA COCONUT CREAM

1 x 400 ml can coconut cream, refrigerated upside down
1 tablespoon maple syrup
1 teaspoon vanilla extract

Scoop the solids of the coconut cream into a bowl, being careful not to add any of the clear liquid (keep this for using in smoothies, sauces and curries). Add the maple syrup and vanilla extract, then use a hand mixer on high speed to whisk until thick and well combined. Store in an airtight container in the fridge for up to 5 days.

Whether it's part of breakfast or used to top a dessert, this is a fantastic coulis recipe that works with any berries and is super quick and easy. Adding a dash of lemon juice along with the lemon zest creates a lovely combination of sweetness and tartness, and also gives the coulis a longer shelf life in the fridge.

MAKES 250 ML (1 CUP)

# BUZZING BERRY COULIS

125 g (1 cup) berries, fresh or frozen and thawed
1 tablespoon maple syrup or honey
1 teaspoon lemon or lime zest, plus a dash of juice (optional)

Using the back of a fork, mash together your choice of berries, the maple syrup or honey and citrus zest in a bowl. Add a dash of juice if you like, then set aside in the fridge overnight. Enjoy immediately or store in an airtight container in the fridge for up to 7 days.

Whipped vanilla coconut cream, page 211

Kick-ass cookie crumb, page 214

Buzzing berry coulis, page 211

Roasted strawberries, page 210

Rad raw chocolate, page 210

Used to sprinkle, top or coat, this is one versatile sweet-treat staple. I like making it in bulk so I always have something to add to healthy desserts when those sweet cravings kick in!

MAKES 130 G (1 CUP)

# KICK-ASS COOKIE CRUMB

80 g (½ cup) macadamia nuts, roughly chopped
30 g (½ cup) shredded coconut
2 tablespoons coconut oil or butter, melted
1 tablespoon maple syrup

Preheat the oven to 180°C and line a baking tray with baking paper.

Place all the ingredients in a bowl and mix everything together well. Spread the mixture across the prepared baking tray and bake for 5–10 minutes, until golden and aromatic. Store in an airtight container in the fridge for up to 2 weeks.

I have included these fried maple banana slices in this section as they are not only a perfect snack on their own but also make an amazing addition to other desserts such as pancakes, or as a topping for muffins. Try topping the banana slices with my Cookie crumb (above) or coating them with my melted Rad raw chocolate (see page 210) for a simple but delicious treat.

SERVES 2

# FRIED MAPLE BANANA SLICES

2 tablespoons coconut oil
1 slightly under-ripe banana, thickly sliced
1 tablespoon maple syrup
½ teaspoon ground cinnamon

Melt the coconut oil in a frying pan over medium heat. Add the banana slices to the pan and cook for 1–2 minutes on each side, until just caramelised – be careful not to overcook them as they can turn to mush! Remove from the heat and set aside.

Meanwhile, in a small bowl whisk together the maple syrup and 1 tablespoon of warm water. Pour this mixture over the cooked bananas, sprinkle with the cinnamon and enjoy.

This is a great jam to have on hand for when those sweet cravings hit – try it spread on my Coconut and blueberry loaf (see page 64).

MAKES ABOUT 500 G (2 CUPS)

# STRAWBERRY/BLUEBERRY JAM

600 g strawberries, hulled, or blueberries, fresh or frozen and thawed

30 g (½ cup) shredded coconut

2 tablespoons maple syrup

pinch of salt

Place all the ingredients and 3 tablespoons of water in a blender and pulse until smooth. Pass the jam through a fine sieve and store in an airtight container in the fridge for up to 1 week or in the freezer for up to 3 months.

I don't know about you, but I find dessert cravings come on quickly and suddenly. And that's what makes this one-mug self-saucing pudding so perfect. If you're at work when those cravings hit the most, then why not take the ingredients to the office and enjoy it as a mid-afternoon snack?

SERVES 1

# SPEEDY SELF-SAUCING PUDDING

55 g (½ cup) almond meal

2 tablespoons coconut sugar

3 tablespoons cacao powder

½ vanilla pod, split and seeds scraped (optional)

pinch of ground cinnamon (optional)

pinch of sea salt

2 eggs, whisked

80 ml (⅓ cup) Vanilla Almond Milk or Homemade Coconut Milk (see pages 252–253)

**To serve (optional)**

Whipped Vanilla Coconut Cream (see page 211)

Kick-ass Cookie Crumb (see opposite)

In a mug or ramekin, mix together the almond meal, coconut sugar, cacao powder, vanilla seeds, cinnamon and salt with a fork. Stir in the whisked egg and milk and whisk together to form a thick, chocolatey batter.

Microwave on high for 60 seconds, or until puffed up and springy to the touch (if you have a really powerful microwave you may want to check after 30 seconds).

Serve straight away, either on its own or with a dollop of my whipped vanilla coconut cream and a sprinkling of my kick-ass cookie crumb.

## TIP

No microwave? No problem. It might not be quite so super speedy, but you can just as easily bake this in a preheated 180°C oven for 10–15 minutes, until lovely and springy!

# FOOD FOR THOUGHT

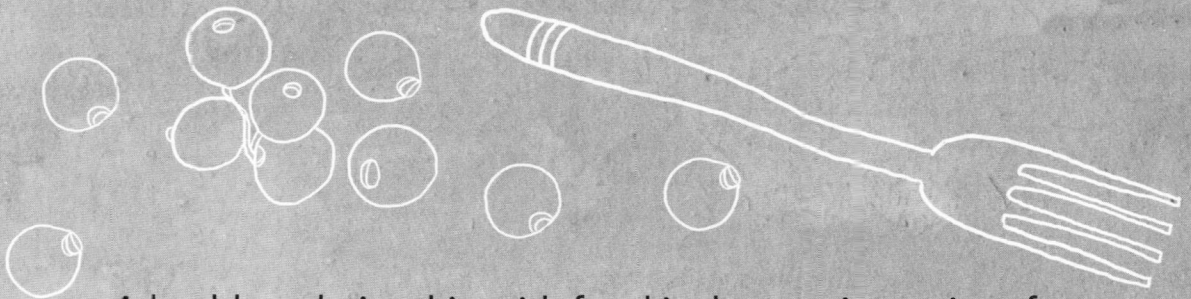

A healthy relationship with food is the starting point of any truly healthy lifestyle. Food is our fuel source and something we need every day in order to survive and thrive – there is no avoiding it. I believe this relationship starts with respecting ourselves enough to consume the foods that allow us to shine both inside and out. It also means eliminating any negative connotations or associations surrounding our food choices.

The connection between what we eat and how we feel is quite profound. There are mood-boosting foods that release happiness hormones, such as serotonin, as well as foods that we as individuals are drawn to from an emotional perspective and find comforting in times of stress and sadness. I think it is important to let yourself have moments of celebrating these foods, even though they may not always fall within my 'eating clean' principles. I'm not suggesting they become everyday foods, rather I'm saying that in order to retain a sustainable, healthy relationship with food, it's okay to sometimes give in to these urges. That doesn't mean you have failed; it means you are human. The reason I have included so many healthy sweet-treat recipes in this book is to give you guys more nutrient-dense options for when you're looking to celebrate, reward or nourish yourselves – in good times or in bad. I'd rather you celebrate real food ingredients when indulging, instead of processed foods, which can be addictive and destructive.

For as long as I can remember I have always loved lemon tarts and slices. There is something so incredible about the flavour and texture combo of that crunchy base and luscious lemon filling. This book is all about easy, and this recipe is no exception.

MAKES ABOUT 12

# EASY AS LEMON SLICE

## Base
100 g (1 cup) almond meal
3 tablespoons almond butter
1 tablespoon maple syrup or honey
2 tablespoons coconut oil
1 vanilla pod, split and seeds scraped
1 teaspoon baking powder
generous pinch of sea salt

## Filling
4 eggs
125 ml (½ cup) maple syrup or honey
zest of 1 lemon plus juice of 2 lemons
3 tablespoons coconut flour
pinch of sea salt

## To serve (optional)
Whipped Vanilla Coconut Cream (see page 211)
Kick-ass Cookie Crumb (see page 214)

Get started by preheating the oven to 180°C and lining a 30 x 20 cm baking tin with baking paper.

For the base, pulse all the ingredients in a food processor to a crumb-like consistency. Using your fingers, press the mixture evenly into the base of the prepared tin, then prick a few holes in it with a fork. Bake for 10 minutes, or until golden.

Meanwhile, make the filling by placing all the ingredients in a food processor and blending together until smooth.

When the base is cooked, remove the tin from the oven and pour the lemon filling evenly over the top, then return to the oven and bake for a further 15 minutes, or until the filling has just set (you want it to still retain a little wobble when you give it a gentle shake).

Remove from the oven and leave on a wire rack to cool completely and firm up. To serve, cut into thick slices and top with my whipped vanilla coconut cream or a handful of my kick-ass cookie crumb, if you like, or enjoy it just as it is. Yum!

## TIP

This is a great dessert to freeze. Simply portion it up, pop the slices into separate freezer bags and enjoy up to 3 months down the track.

HAPPINESS in every bite!

These are my healthy interpretation of those famous peanut butter cups you can find in the shops – they're every bit as tasty and are a great way of using my lovely raw chocolate. You'll see I've given the flavours a bit of a mix-up here too, so there should now be a delicious nut butter cup out there for everyone!

MAKES 12 REGULAR-SIZED OR 6 LARGE CUPS

# LUKEY'S LOVELY NUT BUTTER CUPS

1 x quantity Rad Raw Chocolate (see page 210)

### Peanut butter filling
3 tablespoons peanut butter

### Berry burst filling
1 handful of your favourite frozen berries
1 tablespoon shredded coconut, plus extra for garnish

### Terrific turmeric
3 tablespoons macadamia butter
½ vanilla pod, split and seeds scraped
½ teaspoon ground cinnamon
pinch of ground turmeric, plus extra for garnish

### Coffee crunch filling
3 tablespoons almond butter
1 tablespoon ground espresso coffee
1 teaspoon roasted coffee beans, crushed, plus extra whole beans, for garnish

Line a regular 12-hole or large 6-hole muffin tin with paper cases.

Melt down the rad raw chocolate in a small saucepan over low heat, stirring as you go, until thick and creamy.

Make your filling of choice by putting your filling ingredients in a small bowl and stirring to combine (if you're making peanut butter cups then there's nothing to do here!).

Fill the paper cases one-third of the way up with the melted chocolate, then transfer to the freezer and leave to set.

Once set, spoon ½ teaspoon of your chosen filling over each chocolate base. Remelt the chocolate, then pour over the filling to cover. Top each with a little sprinkling of your chosen garnish (or leave plain if making peanut butter cups), then return to the freezer until set. Enjoy straight away or transfer to an airtight container and keep in the fridge for up to 2 weeks or in the freezer for up to 3 months.

## TIP
Each filling makes enough for six large or 12 regular-sized cups. So, if you decide to make all four flavours, reduce each filling recipe by three-quarters.

When we used to go camping as kids, we would stuff bananas with chocolate, wrap them in foil and cook them over the open fire. Delicious! This healthy take on my childhood favourite not only tastes fantastic but can also be made in the comfort of your own home. It's a great way to use up bananas that are close to being wasted because they're over-ripe.

SERVES 2

# FULLY LOADED BANANA LOVE BOATS

2 very ripe bananas
65 g (½ cup) Rad Raw
  Chocolate (see page 210),
  broken into pieces
3 tablespoons shredded
  coconut

Preheat the oven to 220°C and line a baking tray with baking paper.

Make a slit through the skin of the bananas along one side – being sure not to cut or open all the way through to the other side of the flesh. Use your fingers to peel the skin open a little, then stuff the slits with the raw chocolate pieces.

Wrap each banana in a sheet of foil to cover completely, then arrange on the lined baking tray. Bake for 15–20 minutes, until the skins are black.

Remove the bananas from the oven and leave them to cool slightly, then tear away the foil, open up the skins and sprinkle over the shredded coconut to serve. Enjoy!

## TIP

For something a bit different (but equally tasty), instead of the raw chocolate try filling the bananas with 3 tablespoons of your favourite nut butter and sprinkling over 2 tablespoons of cacao nibs when serving in place of the shredded coconut.

Who doesn't love a generous slice of apple pie served with a dollop of cold cream? This recipe is the perfect pie hack for those not wanting to waste time with a fiddly, time-consuming pastry, as the one used here can be made in seconds. Enjoy this with family and friends at your next get-together!

SERVES 6–8

# EASY PEASY APPLE PIE

coconut oil, for greasing

4 granny smith apples, cored, halved and sliced into thin discs

4 eggs

200 ml Vanilla Almond Milk or Homemade Coconut Milk (see pages 252–253)

2 tablespoons maple syrup or honey

1 x quantity Kick-ass Cookie Crumb (see page 214)

Whipped Vanilla Coconut Cream (see page 211), to serve

## Base

100 g (1 cup) almond or hazelnut meal

160 g (1 cup) macadamia nuts

1 egg

3 tablespoons coconut oil or butter, melted

1 tablespoon maple syrup or honey

2 teaspoons ground cinnamon

1 vanilla pod, split and seeds scraped

½ teaspoon ground nutmeg

Preheat the oven to 180°C and grease a 24 cm pie dish generously with coconut oil.

To make the base, pulse all the ingredients together in a food processor to form a dough. Remove the dough and shape into a ball, then roll it between two sheets of baking paper, to a thickness of about 3 mm.

Remove the top layer of baking paper and place the pie dish upside-down on top of the dough, then flip it over so that the dough ends up in the dish. Press the pastry into the edge of the dish with your fingers, trimming off any overlap and patching up any areas that need it with the excess. Bake in the oven for 5 minutes until par-cooked and lightly golden. Set aside to cool slightly.

Layer the apple slices over the pastry. Whisk the eggs, milk and maple syrup or honey together in a bowl to combine, then pour the mixture evenly over the apples. Bake for 35 minutes, or until the apple slices are nicely golden. Remove from the oven, scatter over the cookie crumb and bake for a further 4 minutes, or until the crumb is golden.

Remove the pie from the oven and leave to cool slightly. Serve warm or cold, topped with a dollop of whipped vanilla coconut cream.

## TIP

This pie also works really well with other fruits, so have a play around with what you have in your fruit bowl. Sliced pear, raspberries and strawberries work really well together, for example.

Birthdays are a time for celebrating with good food, but there is no reason why the cake can't be healthy! This recipe highlights how you can make a birthday cake with just a few simple ingredients, including the humble sweet potato; it's the perfect ingredient to give the cake body and awesome flavour!

SERVES 10–12

# THE HEALTHIEST BIRTHDAY CAKE YOU'LL EVER MAKE

200 g sweet potato, peeled and cut into chunks
160 g (2 cups) cashew or macadamia nuts, soaked for 1 hour
120 g (1 cup) cacao powder
1 teaspoon vanilla extract
125 ml (½ cup) maple syrup or honey
pinch of sea salt
250 ml (1 cup) Whipped Vanilla Coconut Cream (see page 211), to serve
120 g (1 cup) Crunchy Cacao and Coconut Clusters (see page 56), to serve

**Base**
200 g (2 cups) hazelnut or almond meal
2 tablespoons coconut sugar
125 ml (½ cup) coconut oil or melted butter

Preheat the oven to 180°C. Grease and line a baking tray and a 22 cm springform cake tin with baking paper.

Arrange the sweet potato on the baking tray in an even layer and roast for 30–45 minutes, until lovely and soft. Remove from the oven and leave to cool slightly, then whiz to a puree in a food processor.

To make the base, put the hazelnut or almond meal, coconut sugar and coconut oil or butter in a bowl and mix well to form a nice sticky paste. Using your fingers, press the mixture firmly and evenly into the base of the prepared cake tin, then transfer to the freezer for 10 minutes to firm up.

Drain the nuts and place in a food processor, along with the sweet potato, cacao, vanilla, maple syrup or honey and salt. Blitz until creamy, smooth and free of lumps (you may need to add 1–2 tablespoons of water to loosen things up a little as you go).

Remove the tin from the freezer, pour the sweet potato mixture over the base and spread evenly. Transfer to the fridge and leave for at least 1½ hours to chill and set.

When ready to serve, spread the whipped vanilla coconut cream over the top of the cake in an even layer and arrange the cacao and coconut clusters to form a pretty ring shape. You're good to go!

## TIP

This cake will keep in the fridge for up to 1 week or in the freezer for up to 3 months.

When I was a kid and went to birthday parties, my favourite food was always the chocolate crackles. I loved how yummy and chocolatey they were! Now, while the flavours here may be a bit more grown up, the crackles are no less tasty. To make them extra fun, put them in paper cupcake liners to set. I've used macadamia nuts here but walnuts or pecans work really well, too!

MAKES ABOUT 20

# CHOCOLATE AND COCONUT CRACKLES

3 tablespoons coconut oil

80 ml (⅓ cup) maple syrup or honey

125 g almond or peanut butter

1 vanilla pod, split and seeds scraped

120 g (2 cups) shredded coconut

1 tablespoon chia seeds

60 g (½ cup) cacao powder

3 tablespoons chopped pecans

3 tablespoons chopped macadamia nuts

Melt the coconut oil in a large saucepan over low heat. Stir in the maple syrup or honey and nut butter, then add the remaining ingredients and stir them through gently until everything is nicely combined. Remove from the heat.

Heap tablespoons of the mixture onto a baking tray or large plates and transfer to the fridge to set.

## TIP

Any extras can be popped into an airtight container and kept in the freezer for up to 3 months to be enjoyed at a later date.

## HEALTH BOOST

Cacao is packed with the mineral magnesium – which can relieve muscle soreness and help keep us cool, calm and collected – while coconut is a wonderful source of natural fat, making it a great addition to a healthy diet.

When I was growing up, there was the most incredible bakery at the end of my street. One thing I always looked forward to was one of their jam tarts – I often got one if I was travelling around doing errands with Mum, as a treat for being good. This clean-living take on those tarts is every bit as rewarding, and they pretty much melt in the mouth!

MAKES 12

# STRAWBERRY JAM TARTS

50 g (½ cup) coconut flour
100 g (¾ cup) arrowroot or tapioca flour, plus extra for dusting
pinch of sea salt
2 tablespoons coconut sugar
50 g butter or 2½ tablespoons coconut oil, chilled and cut into cubes, plus extra for greasing
2 eggs
250 g (1 cup) Strawberry Jam (see page 215)

Combine the flours, salt and coconut sugar in a bowl, add the chilled butter or coconut oil and rub it in with your fingertips until the mixture resembles fine breadcrumbs. Make a well in the centre of the mixture, add the eggs and mix together with your hands to form a sticky dough.

Tip the dough onto a floured work surface and knead briefly to form a ball, then cover in plastic wrap and leave to rest in the fridge for 20 minutes.

Preheat the oven to 200°C and grease a 12-hole muffin tin with a little coconut oil.

Once rested, remove the pastry from the fridge and roll it out between two sheets of baking paper to a thickness of 2 mm. Using a sharp knife or a round pastry cutter, cut the pastry into large circles just bigger than the muffin holes. Gently place the pastry circles in the muffin tin and press into the edges, making sure to cover the sides.

Spoon a tablespoon of strawberry jam into the centre of each tart, then transfer to the oven and bake for 10 minutes, or until beautiful and golden. Transfer the tarts to a wire rack and leave to cool completely before serving (don't be tempted to try these early, as the jam gets extremely hot!).

## HEALTH BOOST

Did you know that good fats like coconut oil can slow down the release of sugars into your bloodstream? That's why all my sweet treats have a good-quality source of fat in them, to help keep your energy levels as balanced as possible.

I love these bite-sized chocolate and raspberry morsels. Not only do they celebrate two of my favourite flavours, but they also provide a fun new take on popcorn for the kids!

SERVES 6

# CHOC-RASPBERRY BOMBS

200 g fresh raspberries
1 tablespoon maple syrup
90 g (1 cup) desiccated coconut
2 medjool dates, pitted
3 tablespoons coconut oil, melted
125 g (1 cup) Rad Raw Chocolate (see page 210)

Line a baking tray with baking paper.

Put the raspberries, maple syrup, desiccated coconut, dates and coconut oil in a food processor and pulse together briefly to form a thick, chunky paste.

Roll the mixture into walnut-sized balls using your hands and insert a toothpick into the centre of each. Arrange the skewered balls on the prepared baking tray and transfer to the freezer for 15–30 minutes to chill and firm up.

Meanwhile, melt down the rad raw chocolate in a small saucepan over low heat, stirring as you go, until thick and creamy.

Once chilled and using the toothpicks to hold, dunk the balls into the melted chocolate to coat them completely. Place the coated balls back on the baking tray and return to the freezer for 5–10 minutes, or until the chocolate has set. Enjoy straight away, or keep in an airtight container in the fridge for up to 1 week or in the freezer for up to 1 month.

## TIP

This super-versatile recipe can also be made using strawberries, blackberries or even cherries in place of the raspberries.

Roast peaches with coconut cream and nut crumble

Strawberries and cream cups

This delicious and incredibly easy dessert celebrates the most gorgeous of stone fruit: the peach. I really encourage you to try this dish the next time peaches are in season – I'm sure you'll fall in love with both its simplicity and taste!

SERVES 4

# ROAST PEACHES WITH COCONUT CREAM AND NUT CRUMBLE

4 peaches, halved and stones removed

80 ml (⅓ cup) Whipped Vanilla Coconut Cream (see page 211)

65 g (½ cup) Kick-ass Cookie Crumb (see page 214)

Preheat the oven to 180°C and line a baking tray with baking paper.

Arrange the peach halves on the prepared baking tray in an even layer and roast in the oven for 20 minutes, or until soft and caramelised. Leave to cool slightly, then divide the peach halves among bowls, dollop over the vanilla coconut cream and sprinkle over the cookie crumb to finish. Enjoy!

I love this recipe as it's a really easy way of whipping up a delicious dessert using my sweet staples. The combination of flavours and textures here is just perfect and reminds me of the classic strawberries and cream lollies I used to enjoy as a kid!

SERVES 2

# STRAWBERRIES AND CREAM CUPS

125 ml (½ cup) Whipped Vanilla Coconut Cream (see page 211)

125 g (½ cup) Roasted Strawberries (see page 210), cooled

3 tablespoons Kick-ass Cookie Crumb (see page 214)

Layer the three ingredients in jars or glass tumblers. Enjoy straight away or, better still, transfer to the fridge and leave to chill for 20 minutes before serving.

While I love the savoury flavours of Mexico, the cuisine also has some wonderful sweet dishes. Here is my healthy take on one of my favourites: the churro. I can't get enough of these cinnamon-y log-shaped doughnuts, especially when dipped into melted chocolate!

SERVES 4–6

# MEXICAN CHURROS WITH MELTED RAW CHOCOLATE

120 g unsalted butter or 120 ml coconut oil
pinch of sea salt
100 g (1 cup) almond meal
100 g (¾ cup) arrowroot or tapioca flour
½ teaspoon baking powder
3 eggs, beaten
1 tablespoon ground cinnamon
200 g (1 cup) superfine coconut sugar
coconut oil, for deep-frying
125 g (1 cup) Rad Raw Chocolate (see page 210)

Add the butter or oil, salt and 250 ml (1 cup) of water to a large saucepan and bring to the boil over medium heat. Using a wooden spoon, stir in the almond meal, flour and baking powder and mix together well to form a smooth, ball-shaped dough. Transfer to a bowl and set aside to cool.

Once cool, add the dough to an electric mixer fitted with a paddle attachment. On medium speed, add the eggs one at a time, beating until incorporated after each addition, until the mixture is light and fluffy. Set aside in the fridge for 30 minutes to rest, then spoon the dough into a piping bag fitted with a 2 cm nozzle or a freezer bag with a hole cut into one of the bottom corners.

Half-fill a heavy-based saucepan with coconut oil and set over medium heat. Heat the oil to 180°C. To test if it is hot enough, simply drop a small piece of the dough into the oil – if it sizzles and bubbles you're good to go.

Using a small, sharp knife to cut the dough, pipe four 10 cm lengths into the oil. Deep-fry for 1–2 minutes, until golden brown. Remove the churros using a slotted spoon and transfer to paper towel to drain. Repeat with the remaining dough, being mindful not to overcrowd the pan.

Meanwhile, melt the rad raw chocolate in a saucepan over low heat, stirring as you go, until thick and creamy.

Combine the cinnamon and coconut sugar in a shallow bowl.

To serve, dust the churros with the cinnamon-sugar mixture, arrange on a platter and accompany with bowls of the melted chocolate sauce for dipping.

## TIP

As it's being used to give the churros a delicate coating, you really want to use a superfine coconut sugar here. If you can't find a very fine one, just give some of the ordinary stuff a whiz in a food processor and you'll be fine.

Sometimes the simplicity of a chocolate ganache tart says it all. I love making this healthy reinvention of the classic crowd-pleaser with its chewy macaroon base as one large tart, though it's also fun to mix it up and make it as little individual tarts for enjoying with family and friends.

SERVES 8–10

# GORGEOUS GANACHE TART

300 g Rad Raw Chocolate
(see page 210), melted
pinch of salt
250 ml (1 cup) coconut
cream

**Almond–coconut base**
2 egg whites, at room
temperature
2 tablespoons coconut
oil or butter
125 ml (½ cup) maple syrup
1 vanilla pod, split and
seeds scraped
120 g (2 cups) shredded
coconut
100 g (1 cup) almond meal

**To serve (optional)**
cacao powder
toasted coconut flakes
fresh berries

Preheat the oven to 180°C. Grease and line a 26 cm fluted tart tin or pie dish with baking paper.

To make the almond–coconut base, combine all the ingredients in a bowl and mix well by hand, or simply place the ingredients in a food processor and pulse until well combined and a dough consistency forms.

Spoon the mixture into the prepared tin and use your fingers to press it into the base and side in an even layer. Bake for 25–30 minutes, until golden brown, then remove from the oven and set aside to cool.

Melt down the rad raw chocolate in a small saucepan over low heat, stirring as you go, until thick and creamy. Add the salt and stir in the coconut cream until well combined, then remove from the heat and pour over the cooled base. Refrigerate for at least 1 hour for the filling to set.

When ready to serve, leave the tart at room temperature for 5 minutes before cutting with a warm knife. Enjoy as it is, or dust with a little cacao powder or scatter over some toasted coconut flakes or a few fresh berries if you like things a bit fancier.

These super-simple cookies are the perfect afternoon snack – they're quick, easy and taste great. Make them for the kids for when they get home from school or whip up a batch to enjoy with a cuppa in the late afternoon.

MAKES 24

# BLUEBERRY KISSES

190 g (2 cups) blanched
   almond flour
pinch of sea salt
½ teaspoon baking powder
3 tablespoons coconut oil
2 tablespoons maple syrup
3 tablespoons Blueberry
   Jam (see page 215)

In a food processor, combine the almond flour, salt and baking powder. Pulse in the coconut oil and maple syrup until a sticky dough forms. Remove from the food processor and, using your hands, bring the dough together to form a smooth ball. Set aside in the fridge for 20 minutes to firm up slightly.

Preheat the oven to 180°C and line two baking trays with baking paper.

Using about a tablespoon of dough at a time, form the dough into little round cookies and place them on the prepared trays. Press your thumb into the centre of each cookie to make an indentation and place ½ teaspoon of the blueberry jam in each well.

Bake in the oven for 8–10 minutes, until golden brown. Allow to cool on the baking trays before tucking in.

Store in an airtight container in the fridge for up to 7 days or in the freezer for up to 3 months.

## TIPS

Almond flour is a refined, blanched version of almond meal and works better with some baking recipes. You can still use almond meal in the recipe, it will just produce a coarser finished result.

For delicious chocolate kisses, try melting down a little of my Rad Raw Chocolate (see page 210) and adding spoonfuls to the centre of each kiss in place of the jam.

It is no secret that I absolutely *love* brownies. Easy, chocolatey and fudgey, they are pretty much everything I love about dessert in one package. These particular brownies are packed with sweet potato and beetroot, which help bring a lot of extra nutrients to the table. The kids will never know quite how good for them these really are!

MAKES 9

# BRILLIANT BROWNIES WITH BLUEBERRY COULIS

½ sweet potato (about 120 g), peeled and cut into chunks

1 beetroot (about 150 g) peeled and finely grated

100 g (1 cup) almond meal

60 g (½ cup) cacao powder

185 ml (¾ cup) coconut oil, melted

125 ml (½ cup) maple syrup

4 eggs

1 vanilla pod, split and seeds scraped

250 ml (1 cup) Buzzing Berry Coulis (see page 211)

Preheat the oven to 180°C and line a baking tray and a 20 cm square baking tin with baking paper.

Arrange the sweet potato on the baking tray in an even layer and roast for 30–45 minutes, until lovely and soft. Remove from the oven and leave to cool slightly, then whiz to a puree in a food processor.

Put the pureed sweet potato in a bowl together with the remaining ingredients, except the coulis, and mix together really well to form a batter.

Pour the brownie batter evenly into the prepared baking tin and bake in the oven for 20–25 minutes, or until the top is looking firm and crunchy and gives a little resistance when lightly touched (be sure you don't overcook them as you want them to be nice and gooey in the middle).

Remove from the oven and leave to cool in the tin, then cut into nine pieces. Serve topped with my buzzing blueberry coulis. Leftover brownies can be kept in an airtight container in the fridge for up to 7 days.

I LOVE this as the PERFECT pre-workout fuel!

This is such a fun slice to make because you can get really creative when it comes to decorating the top with the melted chocolate! The addition of the sticky nut butter is what gives this dish its lovely fudgey, cookie-dough consistency.

MAKES 8–10

# MACADAMIA AND COCONUT COOKIE DOUGH SLICE

160 g (1 cup) macadamia
nuts, roughly chopped
125 ml (½ cup) coconut oil
3 tablespoons maple syrup
or honey
55 g (1 cup) coconut flakes,
lightly toasted
250 g macadamia nut or
almond butter
1 tablespoon chia seeds
pinch of sea salt
125 g (1 cup) Rad Raw
Chocolate (see page 210)

Place the macadamia nuts in a bowl and cover with warm water. Leave to soak for 20 minutes, then drain.

Line a baking tray with baking paper.

Place three-quarters of the macadamia nuts in a food processor with the coconut oil and maple syrup or honey and blend together until really smooth. Add the coconut flakes, nut butter, chia seeds and salt and pulse together a few times until incorporated. Spread the mixture out evenly in the prepared baking tray and transfer to the freezer for 30 minutes, or until set firm.

Melt down the rad raw chocolate in a small saucepan over low heat, stirring as you go, until thick and creamy.

Once set, drizzle the melted raw chocolate over the slice base in rough, random lines to create a cool pattern (unleash your inner artist here!). Roughly chop the remaining macadamia nuts and scatter over the slice. Return to the freezer for 5 minutes or so to firm up again.

To serve, cut into squares with a warm knife.

## HEALTH BOOST

As well as being a good source of protein, chia seeds contain loads of omega-3 fatty acids, which are great for our overall wellbeing.

I think all of us can remember enjoying one of these from the corner shop after school during childhood! Just because we choose to eat clean doesn't mean we can't enjoy those famous flavours we know and love, as these 'Twix' biscuits prove!

MAKES 6–8

# THE 'TWIX'

### Base
100 g (⅔ cup) coconut flour
pinch of sea salt
2 tablespoons maple syrup
125 ml (½ cup) coconut oil
    or 120 g butter, at room
    temperature

### Caramel filling
125 g macadamia nut or
    almond butter
3 tablespoons maple syrup
3 tablespoons coconut oil,
    melted
1 vanilla pod, split and
    seeds scraped
generous pinch of sea salt

### Chocolate topping
125 g (1 cup) Rad Raw
    Chocolate (see page 210)
pinch of sea salt (optional)

Preheat the oven to 180°C and line a 20 cm square baking tin with baking paper.

To make the base, combine the coconut flour and salt in a bowl. Stir in the maple syrup until fully combined, then add the coconut oil or butter and mix together with your hands to form a smooth dough. Using your fingers, press the mixture firmly and evenly into the base of the prepared tin, then bake for 10–12 minutes, until golden brown around the edges. Remove from the oven and leave to cool.

For the caramel filling, melt the ingredients together in a saucepan over medium–low heat, stirring gently, until nice and runny. Pour the filling over the cooled base, transfer to the fridge and leave for 30 minutes, or until chilled and set.

To make the chocolate topping, melt down the rad raw chocolate in a small saucepan over low heat, stirring as you go, until thick and creamy.

Once the caramel filling has set, pour the melted chocolate over and smooth the surface. Sprinkle over the salt (if using) and return to the fridge for 30 minutes for the topping to set.

To serve, remove from the fridge and cut into fingers with a warm knife.

Rocky Road is up there as one of my favourite desserts. Crunchy nuts combined with soft marshmallows, all brought together with decadent chocolate goodness – what could be better? I hope you love this version as much as I do!

SERVES 10–12

# RIDIC ROCKY ROAD

500 ml (2 cups) coconut cream
2 tablespoons gelatine powder
250 g (2 cups) Rad Raw Chocolate (page 210),
100 g fresh raspberries
80 g (½ cup) macadamia nuts, crushed

Line a 30 cm x 20 cm baking tin with baking paper.

Warm the coconut cream in a saucepan over medium–low heat, add the gelatine and whisk for 10–15 seconds, until the gelatine has dissolved.

Pour the coconut cream mixture into the prepared baking tin, transfer to the fridge and leave for at least 30 minutes, or until completely set.

Meanwhile, melt down the rad raw chocolate in a small saucepan over low heat, stirring as you go, until thick and creamy.

Once set, lift the 'marshmallow' from the baking tin by pulling up the edges of the baking paper. Cut it into rough chunks (I like to keep the sizes of mine nice and varied to make things interesting).

Line the baking tin with another sheet of baking paper, then scatter over the marshmallow pieces, raspberries and macadamia nuts. Pour over the chocolate and return to the fridge for 30 minutes, or until set, then cut the rocky road into chunky squares and you're good to go.

Nothing says 'afternoon tea' quite like a delicious, chocolatey Tim Tam, though I'd go as far as saying that I think this healthy version of the classic biscuit is even better than the original.

SERVES 10–12

# THE 'TIM TAM'

## Biscuit

100 g (1 cup) almond meal
90 g (⅔ cup) coconut flour
40 g (⅓ cup) cacao powder
pinch of sea salt
3 tablespoons coconut oil
2 eggs
2 tablespoons maple syrup

## Chocolate–cashew cream

300 g (2 cups) cashew nuts,
   soaked for 30 minutes
200 ml coconut cream
2 tablespoons cacao
   powder
2 tablespoons maple syrup

## Chocolate coating

440 g cacao butter or
   coconut oil
240 g (2 cups) cacao
   powder
3 tablespoons maple syrup

Preheat the oven to 160°C and line two large baking trays with baking paper.

To make the biscuit, pulse the almond meal, coconut flour, cacao powder and salt in a food processor until combined. Add the coconut oil, eggs and maple syrup and blitz until everything comes together to form a nice, sticky dough.

Shape the dough into a ball, then roll it between two sheets of baking paper to a thickness of 5 mm. Cut the dough into an even number of rectangles – 10 cm lengths for super-sized 'Tim Tams' or 5 cm lengths for more traditional-sized biscuits.

Arrange the biscuits on one of the prepared baking trays, spacing them out evenly, and bake for 10–15 minutes, until firm and crisp around the edges. Remove from the oven, transfer to a wire rack and leave to cool completely.

For the chocolate–cashew cream, drain the cashew nuts, then place all the ingredients in a food processor and blitz until smooth and creamy with a thick, spreadable texture.

Place one of the biscuits on the other lined baking tray and spread generously with the chocolate-cashew cream. Top with another biscuit, pressing down lightly so the cream fills right out to the edges and using your finger to smooth away any excess. Repeat with the remaining biscuits and cream, then transfer to the fridge for 30 minutes to chill and firm up.

For the chocolate coating, melt the ingredients together in a saucepan over low–medium heat until nice and runny. Remove from the heat and leave to cool slightly.

Now it's time to get coating. Place your biscuits on a wire rack over your baking tray. Using a spoon, pour the melted chocolate over the top of each biscuit (you don't need to pick the biscuits up during this process as the sides will naturally get a good covering from all the chocolate that pours over the top). You can reuse any chocolate that runs off the sides onto the baking tray.

Set the 'Tim Tams' back in the fridge for 30 minutes for the chocolate to set, and then they are ready to enjoy! These 'Tim Tams' will keep in an airtight container in the fridge for up to 2 weeks or in the freezer for up to 3 months.

It's hard to have a Gaytime on your own! Or so says the ad for the famous ice cream, which I think means that this delicious 'Gaytime' cake is perfect for sharing.

SERVES 8–10

# THE 'GAYTIME' CAKE

### Nut–biscuit crunch

1 tablespoon coconut oil, melted
3 tablespoons maple syrup
1 egg
1 teaspoon vanilla extract
pinch of sea salt
¼ teaspoon cream of tartar
½ teaspoon bicarb of soda
80 g (¾ cup) almond meal
45 g (½ cup) desiccated coconut
1½ tablespoons arrowroot or tapioca flour
2 teaspoons Vanilla Almond Milk (see page 252)

### Caramel cream

3 x 270 ml cans coconut cream
125 ml (½ cup) maple syrup
pinch of sea salt
2 teaspoons vanilla extract

### Vanilla sponge cake

6 eggs, separated
125 ml (½ cup) maple syrup
1 tablespoon vanilla extract
125 ml (½ cup) Vanilla Almond Milk (see page 252)
100 g (¾ cup) coconut flour
3 teaspoons baking powder

### Chocolate frosting

1 large ripe avocado
2 teaspoons vanilla extract
60 g (½ cup) cacao powder
3 tablespoons maple syrup
1–2 tablespoons Whipped Vanilla Coconut Cream (see page 211)

For the nut–biscuit crunch, whiz all of the ingredients except the almond milk in a blender until combined. Add the milk and pulse together briefly to form a thick, wet dough. Transfer the mixture to the fridge to chill for at least 30 minutes.

Preheat the oven to 175°C and line a baking tray and a 23 cm springform cake tin with baking paper.

Place heaped tablespoons of the biscuit mixture on the lined tray and press with the back of a fork to flatten into rough rounds. Chill in the fridge for 15 minutes, then bake for 16–18 minutes, until lightly browned. Cool completely on a wire rack, then transfer to a zip-lock bag and crush into small pieces.

To make the caramel cream, bring two-thirds of the coconut cream, the maple syrup and salt to the boil in a saucepan over medium heat. Reduce to a simmer and cook, stirring regularly, for 15–25 minutes, until thick and dark golden in colour. Stir in the vanilla extract and simmer for a further 5 minutes, then pour into a heatproof container and leave to cool in the fridge. Whisk the remaining coconut cream in a bowl until thick. Add 6–8 tablespoons of the cooled caramel sauce a tablespoon at a time, whisking as you go, until the cream is thick with a lovely caramel flavour. Transfer to the fridge to chill.

For the vanilla sponge, whisk the egg whites in a bowl using an electric whisk until soft peaks form. Continue to whisk, adding the maple syrup a tablespoon at a time, until the mixture has tripled in size and formed stiff peaks. Whisk in the vanilla extract, egg yolks and almond milk until thick and aerated. In a separate bowl, combine the coconut flour and baking powder, then add to the egg mixture and whisk on low until combined. Whisk for a further 30–60 seconds on medium–high speed until the batter is light and fluffy, then pour into the prepared cake tin and bake for about 35 minutes, or until lightly golden on top and a skewer inserted into the centre comes out clean. Set aside to cool, then remove the sponge from the tin and cut in half horizontally using a serrated knife. Place one layer on a serving plate and spread over the caramel cream, then place the second layer on top. Place in the freezer for 30 minutes.

For the chocolate frosting, whiz the avocado, vanilla, cacao and maple syrup in a food processor until smooth, then add the whipped coconut cream and blitz for 2–3 minutes, until fluffy. Cover the top of the cake with the chocolate frosting, then sprinkle the nut-biscuit crunch over the top to finish.

# BASICS

I love this dairy-free alternative to regular cow's milk. From starting my day with it in my morning coffee to utilising it in so many of my recipes, it's a great thing to have on hand.

MAKES 1.25 LITRES (5 CUPS)

# VANILLA ALMOND MILK

155 g (1 cup) almonds,
 soaked in water for at
 least 8 hours
1 litre (4 cups) filtered water
1 vanilla pod, split and
 seeds scraped
pinch of sea salt

Drain the soaked nuts and rinse them really well. Place the nuts, filtered water, vanilla and salt in a high-speed blender and blend for 2–3 minutes, or until nice and creamy.

Line a bowl with either a nut milk bag or a piece of muslin, so that the fabric hangs over the edge of the bowl.

Pour the blended nut and water mixture into the bowl. Pick up the edges of the bag or muslin and squeeze out all the milk. Keep the leftover pulp to use in your baking.

Store the milk in an airtight jar in the fridge for up to 4 days, being sure to shake well before each use.

## TIP

To make a cacao nut milk, add 1 tablespoon ground cinnamon, 125 g (1 cup) cacao powder and 4 pitted medjool dates that have been soaked in boiling water for 10 minutes to the blender with the other ingredients. Try experimenting with different types of nuts and mixing nut milks too – I personally love the combination of macadamia and cashew milk.

This is a quick and easy recipe that can be used in addition to, or as a replacement for, the almond milk in many of my recipes. Much lighter than the canned stuff, this coconut milk is perfect for your warm drinks, smoothies and curries.

MAKES 1.25 LITRES (5 CUPS)

# HOMEMADE COCONUT MILK

1 litre (4 cups) filtered water
120 g (2 cups) shredded
coconut
1 vanilla pod, split and
seeds scraped
pinch of sea salt

Pour the filtered water into a saucepan over medium heat and bring to a simmer. Remove from the heat and pour into a blender. Add the shredded coconut, vanilla seeds and salt and blend or pulse on high for 2–5 minutes, or until the liquid becomes thick and creamy.

Line a colander with two large layers of muslin and place over a large bowl. Pour the coconut milk through the lined colander, then pick up the edges of the muslin and squeeze as much liquid as possible out of the coconut into the colander.

Store the coconut milk in an airtight container in the refrigerator for up to 3–4 days, being sure to give it a bit of a shake before use as the solids can settle at the bottom.

I was recently fortunate enough to work with Mickey Trescott, the author of a number of cookbooks on living with autoimmune disease, and she taught me this wonderful passata recipe with no tomatoes! While perfect for those with the particular autoimmune conditions that tomatoes can aggravate it is, most importantly, also simply delicious. Use it in place of your regular passata or tomato sauce.

MAKES ABOUT 1 LITRE (4 CUPS)

# GARLICKY NO-TOMATO PASTA SAUCE

2 tablespoons coconut oil
2 onions, finely chopped
8 garlic cloves, finely chopped
1 large beetroot (about 400 g), peeled and grated
2 carrots, grated
2 celery stalks, grated
1 tablespoon finely chopped oregano leaves
2 tablespoons finely chopped flat-leaf parsley leaves
1 teaspoon sea salt
500 ml (2 cups) vegetable stock (see pages 38–39) or filtered water
juice of 1 lemon

Melt the coconut oil in a saucepan over medium heat, add the onion, garlic, beetroot, carrot and celery and cook for 10–12 minutes, or until all the veg have started to soften and the onion is translucent.

Stir in the oregano, parsley and salt, pour over the stock and bring to the boil. Reduce the heat to a simmer and cook for 20 minutes, or until vegetables are lovely and tender. Set aside to cool, then transfer to a food processor together with the lemon juice and blend until smooth. Store in an airtight container in the fridge for up to 7 days.

I could enjoy this pesto with close to anything … well, maybe not pancakes, but you get the picture! Its zesty, vibrant and bold flavours really sing, and it's so easy to whip up. When making pestos and similar green-style sauces and dressings, you can often utilise whatever green herbs you might have in the fridge. Coriander leaves also work brilliantly in this recipe and can add a lovely Mexican or Asian flavour when paired with the right dish.

MAKES ABOUT 250 G (2 CUPS)

# CHILLI MACADAMIA PESTO

2 bunches of basil, leaves picked

2 bunches of flat-leaf parsley, leaves picked

80 g (½ cup) macadamia nuts

4 garlic cloves, finely chopped

1 long red chilli, roughly chopped

125 ml (½ cup) extra-virgin olive oil

juice of 1 lemon

1 tablespoon apple cider vinegar

sea salt and freshly ground black pepper

Place all the ingredients in a food processor and pulse together a few times until well combined and to a consistency of your liking – the amount of time you pulse will dictate how chunky or smooth your pesto will be.

Store in an airtight container in the fridge for up to 5 days.

## TIP

Anyone who knows me and my cooking style knows I absolutely *love* the heat from chilli, which is why I don't often remove the seeds from fresh ones when I use them. If you want to cool things down slightly here (or in any of my other recipes), simply deseed the chillies before using.

Garlicky no-tomato pasta sauce, page 254

Chilli macadamia pesto, page 255

I love this simple recipe because it's a nice twist on a familiar favourite – the flavours of the lemon and smoked paprika work brilliantly with the aioli's garlicky creaminess.

MAKES ABOUT 250 G (1½ CUPS)

# LEMON AND SMOKED PAPRIKA AIOLI

1 egg
1 teaspoon dijon mustard
juice of ½ lemon
sea salt
250 ml (1 cup) extra-virgin
   olive oil
2 garlic cloves, finely
   chopped
2 teaspoons smoked
   paprika
freshly ground black
   pepper

Put the egg, mustard, lemon juice and a generous pinch of salt in a food processor and whiz together on low speed for 30 seconds to combine. With the motor still running, slowly pour in the olive oil in a thin stream until it has all been incorporated and the aioli is thick and creamy. (Alternatively, whisk the ingredients together with a hand whisk in a bowl, adding the olive oil in a slow, steady stream as before – it'll just take a lot longer.)

Stir in the garlic and smoked paprika and season with salt and pepper. Store in an airtight container and keep in the refrigerator for up to 7 days.

I could eat guacamole with any meal! These simple Mexican flavours combined with the creamy fat from avocado is up there as one of my favourite dishes!

MAKES ABOUT 250 G (1½ CUPS)

# GORGEOUS GUACAMOLE

2 ripe avocados, mashed
1 garlic clove, grated
1 teaspoon ground cumin
1 teaspoon ground
   coriander
1 teaspoon sweet paprika
1 teaspoon sea salt
zest and juice of 2 limes
zest and juice of 1 lemon
1 bird's eye chilli, deseeded
   and finely chopped
1 tablespoon extra-virgin
   olive oil

Add all the ingredients to a bowl and stir together until well combined. Store in an airtight container in the fridge for up to 3 days.

Some recipes just scream out for a generous dollop of sour cream – baked sweet potato anyone? No worries, with this super-easy recipe I've got you covered.

MAKES 375 ML (1½ CUPS)

# PALEO SOUR CREAM

1 x 400 ml can coconut
   cream
juice of 1 lemon
1 teaspoon apple cider
   vinegar
pinch of salt

Scoop the solid cream from the coconut can into a bowl (keep the clear coconut liquid for smoothies!). Add the lemon juice, apple cider vinegar and salt and whisk together until well combined. Taste and add more lemon juice or salt if necessary, then transfer to an airtight container and store in the fridge for up to 7 days.

I love this simple, nut-based cottage cheese recipe. It's perfect on top of a toasted slice of my broccoli bread (see page 65) with a generous drizzle of lemon juice.

MAKES 250 G (1 CUP)

# PALEO COTTAGE CHEESE

250 ml (1 cup) canned
   coconut milk
juice of 1 lime
pinch of salt
2 teaspoons gelatine
   powder

Warm the coconut milk, lime juice and salt in a saucepan over medium heat. Once lukewarm, whisk in the gelatine powder a little at a time until the gelatine is fully dissolved and the mixture is lump-free. Pour the liquid into a bowl, cover with plastic wrap and leave in the fridge for 2–3 hours until it has thickened.

Transfer to an airtight container and keep in the fridge for up to 7 days.

When ready to serve, tip the chilled mixture into a food processor and pulse briefly to the consistency of cottage cheese.

I love this simple green sauce. In this book, I have paired it with grilled mackerel (see page 176) but it really is super versatile – try it with scrambled eggs, served alongside seafood or tossed through a fresh salad.

MAKES ABOUT 200 G (1½ CUPS)

# GREAT GREMOLATA

3 large handfuls of flat-
   leaf parsley leaves, finely
   chopped
2 garlic cloves, finely
   chopped
3 tablespoons extra-virgin
   olive oil
zest and juice of 2 lemons
generous pinch of salt
pinch of freshly ground
   black pepper

Place all the ingredients in a small bowl, cover with plastic wrap and refrigerate for 1 hour before using. Store in an airtight container and use within 4 days.

Arm yourself with a hand-held blender for this baby, and you'll have some epic mayo on your plate in no time!

MAKES ABOUT 300 G (2 CUPS)

# LESS-THAN-A-MINUTE MAYO

4 egg yolks
2 teaspoons dijon mustard
1 tablespoon apple cider
   vinegar
juice of ½ lemon
400 ml extra-virgin olive oil
sea salt and freshly ground
   black pepper

Place the egg yolks, mustard, vinegar, lemon juice, oil and a pinch of salt in a glass jug or jar and blend with a hand-held blender until smooth and creamy. Season with salt and pepper to taste. Store in the fridge in an airtight container for up to 5 days.

Macadamias would have to be my favourite nut. Not only are they incredibly versatile in breakfasts, salads, desserts and more, they also have a really high level of omega-3s, the good fats we want to give a starring role in our diets.

MAKES 500 G (1½ CUPS)

# MACADAMIA RICOTTA

320 g (2 cups) macadamia
    nuts
juice of 1 lemon
1 teaspoon sea salt
125 ml (½ cup) filtered
    water, plus extra if
    needed

Place all the ingredients in a food processor and puree to a smooth paste, scraping down the sides with a spatula halfway through to ensure that everything gets mixed together well and adding a little extra water if you need to loosen it up a little. Store in an airtight container in the fridge for up to 7 days.

Whether it's on top of a pizza or tossed through a salad, this cashew feta makes for a fantastic dairy-free cheese option.

MAKES 230 G (1½ CUPS)

# CASHEW FETA

155 g (1 cup) cashew nuts,
    soaked in water for at
    least 3 hours
1 garlic clove, roughly
    chopped
2 tablespoons extra-virgin
    olive oil
juice of 1 lemon
sea salt and freshly ground
    black pepper

Drain the soaked nuts and rinse them really well, then place them in a food processor with the garlic, olive oil and lemon juice. Season with salt and pepper and blend until beautifully smooth, adding a dash of water to loosen everything up a little if needed. Store in an airtight container in the fridge for up to 7 days.

Fresh, summery and vibrant, this recipe is one of my favourite ways to celebrate fruit alongside any number of proteins. The creaminess of the avocado really helps balance the sweetness of the pineapple, and the addition of the herbs and spices makes this a winning accompaniment to any dish.

MAKES ABOUT 300 G (2 CUPS)

# PINEAPPLE AND AVOCADO SALSA

¼ pineapple, cut into cubes
2 avocados, cut into cubes
½ bunch of coriander, leaves picked and finely chopped
zest and juice of 1 lemon
2 tablespoons extra-virgin olive oil
1 tablespoon apple cider vinegar
½ long red chilli, deseeded and finely diced
pinch of sea salt
pinch of freshly ground black pepper

Gently mix all the ingredients together in a bowl and set aside for 10 minutes for the flavours to infuse.

This salsa will keep in an airtight container in the fridge for up to 5 days, but it is best eaten fresh.

Tahini is a great source of protein and calcium, as well as vitamin E and a wide range of B vitamins. Whipped up into a flavoursome dressing with turmeric, it makes a wonderful option for coating salad leaves or drizzling over simply sautéed greens.

MAKES ABOUT 500 ML (2 CUPS)

# TURMERIC AND TAHINI DRESSING

270 g (1 cup) tahini
125 ml (½ cup) hot water
2 teaspoons ground turmeric
2 garlic cloves, finely chopped
juice of 1 lemon
2 tablespoons apple cider vinegar
sea salt and freshly ground black pepper

Simply combine all the ingredients in a food processor and blitz until creamy and smooth (if you prefer a runnier dressing, simply add a little extra water). Season with salt and pepper to taste, transfer to an airtight container or jar and keep in the fridge for up to 7 days.

## TIP

Tahini that is made from unhulled sesame seeds is more nutrient-rich than the kind made from hulled seeds, but it is also more bitter. Use what you have to hand or can find at the shops and feel free to tweak the quantity given here until you have a dressing that suits your tastebuds.

This is my take on the very popular green goddess dressing. It's perfect for those wanting to add a little extra vitality to their diets in the shape of additional nutrient-dense veggies and healthy fats.

MAKES ABOUT 500 ML (2 CUPS)

# GREEN GOODNESS DRESSING

1 bunch of flat-leaf parsley, leaves picked
1 bunch of coriander, leaves picked
1 large avocado, roughly chopped
1 zucchini, roughly chopped
2 tablespoons apple cider vinegar
juice of 1 lemon
125 ml (½ cup) extra-virgin olive oil
pinch of sea salt
pinch of freshly ground black pepper

Using a food processor or stick blender, blitz all the ingredients together until well combined, smooth and creamy, adding 1–2 tablespoons of water to loosen the dressing a little if necessary. Store in an airtight container in the fridge for up to 4 days.

We all need to have a go-to salad dressing in our lives, and this one's a cracker! It's quick, simple and flavoursome – everything a dressing (and indeed, all healthy cooking) should be.

MAKES ABOUT 500 ML (2 CUPS)

# GO-TO SALAD DRESSING

250 ml (1 cup) extra-virgin olive oil or avocado oil
juice of 1½ lemons
3 tablespoons apple cider vinegar
1 garlic clove, finely chopped
1 teaspoon dijon mustard
½ teaspoon chilli flakes (optional)
2 tablespoons chopped parsley or basil leaves
1 teaspoon salt

Put all the ingredients in a bowl and whisk by hand until really well combined. Store in a jar in the fridge for up to 3 weeks.

## TIP

Feel free to mix up the herbs for whatever you have to hand.

I just love dukkah! It makes for the perfect last-minute addition to a salad when sprinkled over the top, as well as being a fantastic coating for all sorts of meats, fish and vegetables.

MAKES ABOUT 250 G (2 CUPS)

# MACADAMIA DUKKAH

2 teaspoons coriander seeds

2 teaspoons cumin seeds

2 tablespoons white sesame seeds

200 g (1½ cups) finely chopped macadamia nuts

2 teaspoons dried parsley (optional)

1 teaspoon chilli flakes (optional)

sea salt and freshly ground black pepper

Using a mortar and pestle, grind the coriander seeds, cumin seeds and sesame seeds to a fine powder (or whiz together in a food processor).

Add the chopped macadamias to a dry frying pan over medium heat and gently toast for 2 minutes, then add the ground seeds and toast for a further 2 minutes, until the macadamias are golden brown and the spices are fragrant. Remove from the heat and set aside to cool.

Once cooled stir through the dried parsley and chilli flakes (if using) and season to taste with salt and pepper. Store in an airtight container in the cupboard for up to 1 month.

Vibrant, colourful and spicy, this Mexican seasoning will take your tastebuds on an international culinary journey!

MAKES ABOUT 100 G (1 CUP)

# MEXICAN SEASONING

2 tablespoons sweet paprika

2 tablespoons garlic powder

2 tablespoons onion powder

2 tablespoons hot chilli powder

2 tablespoons cayenne pepper

2 tablespoons ground cumin

2 tablespoons ground coriander

1 tablespoon freshly ground black pepper

1 tablespoon sea salt

Combine all the ingredients in an airtight container and give it a good shake. Store in the pantry for up to 3 months.

This seasoning is super quick and easy to make and is fantastic to have on hand to add flavour, spice and vitality to your cooking – think crispy chicken, beef ribs and rissoles!

MAKES ABOUT 100 G (1 CUP)

# TEXAN SEASONING

2 tablespoons sweet paprika
2 tablespoons chilli powder
2 tablespoons garlic powder
2 tablespoons cayenne pepper
2 tablespoons ground cumin
1 tablespoon sea salt
1 tablespoon coconut sugar

Combine all the ingredients in an airtight container and give it a good shake. Store in the pantry for up to 3 months.

I have really been enjoying the flavours of Indian food lately – not only is turmeric a real superfood, but the depth of flavour that Indian spices give any dish is just incredible. This Indian seasoning is perfect for rubbing over vegetables before roasting! Try crispy oven-roasted cauliflower with this mixture.

MAKES ABOUT 100 G (1 CUP)

# INDIAN SEASONING

2 tablespoons ground coriander
2 tablespoons ground cumin
2 tablespoons chilli flakes
1 tablespoon ground turmeric
½ tablespoon ground ginger
½ tablespoon ground black peppercorns
½ tablespoon ground cardamom
1 teaspoon ground cloves
1 teaspoon ground cinnamon

Combine all the ingredients in an airtight container and give it a good shake. Store in the pantry for up to 3 months.

# THANK YOU!

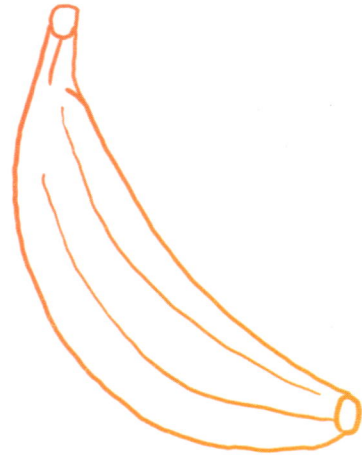

### Lucy Heaver

My regular editor got blessed with a beautiful baby, and I got blessed with you, lovely Lucy. The universe sent me your incredible supportive energy, artistic eye for detail and passion for bringing a beautiful product to life. From our first brainstorm to the printed book, you've imparted your immense commitment and skill to producing something I am profoundly proud of. Our wonderful synergy has truly enabled all readers the gift of Making Healthy Easy for life, and I am so grateful for having you bring this vision to life. Big thanks, Lucy.

### Mary Small

From helping Aussies to *Eat Clean* to this new exciting chapter of *Healthy Made Easy*, Mary you have been such a strong force on making my dreams come true, and for that I am full of gratitude and appreciation. My vision for making easy, healthy and delicious recipes accessible to all was made so much easier with your backing, belief and support each and every step of the journey. I know that without your experience, knowledge and innate skill, I would not be reaching the heights of success I aim for. You're integral to my exciting journey with Plum, and I hope you know it never goes unnoticed or unappreciated. Thanks so much, Mary.

### Mark Roper

I had a sneaky suspicion about you on book one and look, to be honest mate, it was confirmed on book two. You know what you're doing, and you're bloody good at it. Jokes aside, you make the production process of my books both really fun while achieving a professional result. We better not tell the big bosses how much fun we have or they might seperate us in class. You should think about photography as a full-time gig mate, I reckon you'd kill it! Thanks for being a legend.

### Lee Blaylock

I would describe our experience working together on *Eat Clean* as pretty epic, so we had a lot to live up to with this project. You made this sequel such a fun, comforting and relaxing job. I knew each and every shot would be prepared with such finesse and skill that the finished result would be everything I could ask for and more. Your energy on set makes the entire experience something I look forward to. Thanks, Lee.

### Sebastien Nichols

I am trying to work out which title best describes you. I am tossing up between international male model and chef extraordinaire. I think I will go with Model Chef, because lets face it, when you're in the kitchen things get hot, which is why I followed the mantra that if I can't handle the heat, I should get out of the kitchen. Next shoot, can you please not eat all of the delicious leftovers that we need the following days; I don't like having to make three batches of crumble to satiate your appetite, haha! Thanks for the laughs!

### Josh Reekie

Emma warned me that your cooking prowess matched your dry wit and comic timing. Never a truer word spoken. You're fantastic at what you do and provided many great laughs across our time working together. Thanks for stepping into such a key role and making this book come to life with your talent. I hope you love the book mate, thanks for being such a great contributor to what is an awesome result!

### Emma Warren

On day one, I had the widest smile on my face when I heard your 'good morning' from the front door! You brought such zest, life and vibrance to the shoot, and your frank down-to-earth approach at tackling my recipes and bringing them to life is such a hoot! It's a laugh-a-minute experience, and you make me want to be a better cook so I can impress you with my paleo baking creations! Even if it means I have to test recipes every afternoon to be certain you like what you see! Thanks for imparting your knowledge with me to make my skills and this book even better.

### Charlotte Ree

Often not mentioned enough is the key component of getting incredible books like this in the right hands and in the right places, and for this I have you to thank, Charlotte. You are a wonder worker, and I am in awe of your pure commitment to being the best in the industry at what you do. To be working with Plum and having your guidance at the crucial release and beyond, I can only say a huge thanks, and I think we should celebrate with one of your delectable creations, paleo or not!

### Kali Cavanagh

This book wouldn't look the goods without the standout brilliance of our location. Not only was it my home away from home in Melbourne, it was our location for this beautiful book, and a huge thanks must go to you for allowing us to transform your beautiful space with my personality and culinary creations! Thanks Kali, it means the world! Still in love with the blue paint on the front of the house!

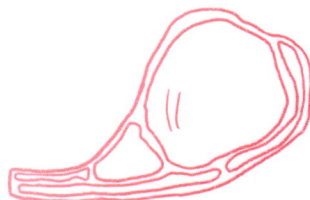

### Simon Davis

Talk about being in sync! *Eat Clean* was epic and we only streamlined and perfected our working relationship with this book. Thanks for having such wonderful hawk eyes with the same easy-going and patient nature that makes editing with you such a joy. You make my life easier and make me a little smarter with every edit note. Cheers buddy!

### Rachel Carter

Rachel, I have you to thank for helping me create a book where every single recipe works, reads correctly and has a positive impact on the reader. The key to a successful cookbook is being 100% certain each and every amazing soul that picks up a copy has a positive experience, and for your eye for detail and attention, I am so grateful.

### Grace West

Writing the easy-to-follow recipes and photographing them in a way that excites both the eye and tastebuds is just one part of creating this book. Creating extraordinary illustrations, intuitive and functional layouts, and formatting all of the diverse and existing content is another, and Grace, I can't thank you enough for doing such an incredible job on this beautiful book. My one brief for the artwork for *Healthy Made Easy* was that it be bright, happy and exciting to look at; well, you achieved all of that and more with your creative genius.

# INDEX

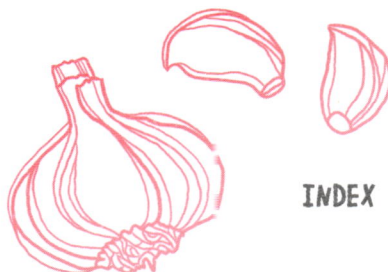

**A Plum book**

First published in 2017 by Pan Macmillan Australia Pty Limited
Level 25, 1 Market Street, Sydney, NSW 2000, Australia,
Level 3, 112 Wellington Parade, East Melbourne, Victoria, Australia 3002

Text copyright © Luke Hines 2017
Photography Mark Roper copyright © Pan Macmillan 2017
Design and illustrations Grace West copyright © Pan Macmillan 2017

The moral right of the author has been asserted.

Design and illustrations by Grace West
Cover design by Kirby Armstrong
Editing by Simon Davis
Index by Frances Paterson
Photography by Mark Roper
Food styling by Lee Blaylock
Food preparation by Emma Warren, Sebastien Nichols and Josh Reekie
Colour reproduction by Splitting Image Colour Studio
Printed and bound in China by Imago Printing International Limited

The publisher would like to thank the following for their generosity in providing props for
the book: Kaz Ceramics, Marmoset Found, Bettina Willner-Browne and Bridget Bodenham.

The publisher would like to thank Kali Cavanagh for providing the location used in this book.

A CIP catalogue record for this book is available from the National Library of Australia.

All rights reserved. No part of this book may be reproduced or transmitted by any person or
entity (including Google, Amazon or similar organisations), in any form or means, electronic or
mechanical, including photocopying, recording, scanning or by any information storage and
retrieval system, without prior permission in writing from the publisher.

We advise that the information contained in this book does not negate personal responsibility
on the part of the reader for their own health and safety. It is recommended that individually
tailored advice is sought from your healthcare or medical professional. The publishers and their
respective employees, agents and authors are not liable for injuries or damage occasioned to
any person as a result of reading or following the information contained in this book.

10 9 8 7 6 5 4 3 2 1